THE
VITALITY
IMPERATIVE

How **connected leaders**
and their teams achieve more
with less time, money,
and stress

MICKEY CONNOLLY

JIM MOTRONI

RICHARD MCDONALD

and the entire
Conversant community

Published by Catalyst Publishing, December 2015

The Connected Leader is a trademark of Conversant Solutions, LLC

Design by Factor Creative
with Erica France and Katie Mingo on behalf of Conversant
Library of Congress Cataloging-in-Publication Data is available.

ISBN: 978-0-9961188-2-8

Dedication

Mickey Connolly

To Fairy Tana, wife, partner and guide, for her fierce devotion to living an honorable life and to Emma Rose and Guy, our extraordinary, inspiring children.

Jim Motroni

To my wife, Debra and my children, Dylan and Ava, who have contributed immeasurably to my vitality, my growth and my life…and tolerated my failure to always return their generosity in kind.

Richard McDonald

To my wife, Amy, thank you for being a confidant and an inspiration to live life with greater presence and heart wide open. I am forever grateful.

Contents

Foreword

I first met Mickey Connolly around 1994 when I was a participant in a leadership class he was leading for managers at Hewlett-Packard Company. At that time, I knew I had connected with someone having genuine curiosity for who I was and what was important to me. By the way, this curiosity was not reserved for myself only– it was extended to each and every person in the room. I remember feeling engaged and more present to the conversation we were all about to have.

Reflecting on the experience now, I realize that seeing us all as valuable and fascinating individuals was the secret to capturing our willingness to be deeply open with the possibility of making even greater contributions as leaders. It was exciting, energizing, fun, and productive. It's no surprise that my organization at the time invested so heavily in not just this training but also in the on-going practice of what was modeled in the class. In no small way, this way of working together contributed to the success and exponential growth of HP's Inkjet business over a ten-year period.

Many others have explored in part and in different ways what Mickey and his co-authors, Jim and Richard, define as *vitality*. Often referred to in the corporate world as well-being, employee satisfaction, ownership, and high performance, most of these related concepts only nibble around the edges of what it really takes for people to connect and commit whole heartedly to each other on behalf of accomplishing great things. With this book, Mickey, Jim, and Richard succeed in giving us something larger and more practical—a useful and catalytic definition of vitality at work and what it takes to protect and expand it over time. Their definition encompasses what it means to be human beings at work, and will help you remove barriers to great and rewarding accomplishments in your organization.

It's taken a while for people to be ready to hear about vitality. Partly, this is because of deeply-seated, erroneous, centuries-old cultural beliefs. These beliefs assert that as humans, we must make tradeoffs between opposing forces: rational individual self-interest vs. seeking the common and collective good. The premise underlying this belief is that the natural order is the individual and that only out of necessity for survival do we give up some of our personal desires in order to be protected. This is simply not true.

In fact, great thinkers, such as Adam Smith, Emile Durkheim, George Herbert Mead, and Humberto Maturana have challenged this underlying assumption with logic and evidence that suggest just the opposite. They reveal we are human *only* because we are socialized. And our nature and the very emergence of our intelligence and well-being are dependent upon our interactions, positive emotions, and solidarity with each other. In short, there is a fundamental human need to live and work together, and to care about one another. The choice between results and community, contribution, and choice is not an either/or. Rather it is a *yes/and*.

The autonomy to pursue a meaningful life only has traction in relationship to each other and a shared purpose. Researchers Edward Deci and Richard Ryan have named universal, co-existing human intrinsic needs: relatedness, competence, and autonomy. *The Vitality Imperative* interprets and expands these essential elements as: *community, contribution, and choice*. In doing so, it further shatters the damaging notion of either/or thinking. Here's the good news of *The Vitality Imperative*: You can both increase organizational vitality *and* dramatically increase business results!

As you read, you will discover the power of making community, contribution, and choice available in any organization. This makes you and your team more innovative because you are having fun. It fosters health because you and your team genuinely care and support one another. And it allows you and your team to accomplish the extraordinary because you are smarter collectively. And because no one has to live in fear and isolation, the best ideas emerge and win in an organization committed to fostering vitality.

As this book reveals, fostering vitality requires keeping seven promises. These promises do not exist only in the cognitive domain. Those committed to keeping them must also develop social, emotional, and physical awareness on the path to becoming connected leaders. For those that do, the rewards are energizing: you and your team successfully achieve the organization's purposes with confidence, joy, and even enthusiasm. Who wouldn't want that every day?

Years ago, while working for a major organization, I was visiting with a colleague about the looming specter of a downsizing and how to best cope. He turned to me and soberly reported, "I know we have great corporate values about respect for the individual and the power of teams, but maybe we can't afford those values right now." This shocking statement still haunts me as a too-common example of our false choices and assumptions. My own research shows it is precisely the times when we are facing daunting problems and conundrums that we must double-down on our beliefs and commitment for what we are in together. This opens new portals to what is possible—and in the process, expands our humanity. As a close research colleague, Dennis Sandow, once said, "To understand performance, follow the joy." As great results can be sensed even before they arrive, I invite the reader to let joy, interest, and positive energy guide your own path to greater organizational vitality.

I cannot overemphasize that what is outlined in the following pages addresses what all human beings want—and what all organizations need. It is deceptively simple, but not necessarily a template easy to practice. Peak performance, thriving, and achieving – all these are both reason for and benefit from *The Vitality Imperative*. No organization, if it wishes to succeed, flourish, and sustain over time, can afford to ignore this call to action. You can't either.

Anne Murray Allen, DSocSci

September 2015

Anne Murray Allen is a Global Partner with Conversant, specializing in organization design, collaboration, and integration. She previously served in executive positions within Hewlett-Packard (HP), at Willamette University, and with her own consulting practice. She has worked with clients such as Babcock & Wilcox, CH2M Hill, Lockheed Martin, Port of Portland, and The Nature Conservancy. Anne has taught graduate level management classes and has presented at conferences around the world. She co-authored the 2005 *Reflections Journal* article, "The Nature of Social Collaboration: How Work Really Gets Done," and is published in the July 2012 edition of *OD Practitioner* on culture integration when merging organizations. She is a past recipient of an American Society of Training and Development (ASTD) Torch Award. Anne is also a past trustee of the D.C.-based, non-profit Millennium Institute and is currently a member of The Academy for Systemic Change.

Author's Note

We are members of *Conversant* (**conversant.com**), a consulting firm researching and sharing how human connectivity shapes organizational performance. We say more about our practice at the end of the book.

The Vitality Imperative is based on our collective experiences and those of our colleagues and clients over the last thirty years. Please note, however, that the final chapter is a fictional story. While it is inspired by real people and events neither the characters nor the organization in which they work is real.

The Vitality Imperative is intended for organizational leaders who want to produce great results with less time, money and stress. We have found that management practices in large organizations around the world are inconsistent with the nature of being human. As Daniel Pink has said, "What science knows is not what business does" and that makes everything harder than necessary. We think it is time to fix that.

We intend this experience for readers:

- You think about causes of performance most people fail to consider.
- You notice things most leaders fail to notice.
- You take actions most leaders do not.
- You produce better results with less time, money and stress.

We would love to hear from you about your reactions to and uses of the information coming your way. We are reachable at ***mickjimrich@conversant.com***.

Mickey Connolly, Jim Motroni, and Richard McDonald

20 September 2015

THE VITALITY IMPERATIVE:

It Starts with a Choice

The prime requirement for achieving any aim,
including quality, is joy in work.

—W. Edwards Deming

First and foremost leadership is about being a human being.
The future world will be much more purpose- and values-driven,
so we want leaders that clearly understand this. It's important to make
people feel more comfortable working in situations where the win-win
is not driven just by your shareholder but by all stakeholders,
and that requires a different skill set.

—Paul Polman, CEO, Unilever

Promises are the uniquely human way of ordering the future.

—Hannah Arendt

Pam is quitting.

"I don't know what I'll do next," she says, "I am leaving because almost anything will be better than this."

A highly regarded manager at one of the largest corporations in the world, Pam is talented, well-compensated, and has much of her career ahead of her.

"We've gone through years of trying to do more with less. It has not worked. We move from acquisitions to layoffs to demanding more from overwhelmed employees who begin to hate their work. I don't want to be part of that toxic cycle any longer. There has to be a better way to lead an organization."

Pam's company has experienced sporadic increases in productivity per employee, but they've done it by demanding more output, not improving how work gets done. Productivity numbers are now in rapid decline and high performers are on their way out the door.

Pam's company is learning the hard way that increasing stress is not a sustainable source of productivity improvement.

And Now for Something Completely Different

Susan is not quitting—nor does she want to.

"I love my work, and it's not just because we are so successful," she says. "I like how we are successful: our CEO actually believes sustainable success needs a smart business model, co-created and implemented by energized employees. Where I used to work, we assessed employee engagement a lot, but it never really improved. Here, we don't just assess engagement—we cause it."

Like Pam, Susan is talented, well compensated, and has much of her career ahead of her. And she loves her company.

"You know what else I love?" she asks. "Both my daughters say they would be proud to work here."

So, the billion-dollar question is, what's the difference between Pam and Susan's organizations?

Susan's organization is achieving more with less time, money, and stress. And that is the story of vitality.

What Is Vitality?

The Vitality Imperative is about how work gets done. From our experiences with more than four hundred organizations on six continents, we are now certain that Susan's vitality work culture produces more great achievement with less time, money, and stress than Pam's.

The definition of "vitality" includes "the capacity to live, grow or develop; the presence of intellectual and physical vigor; energy." What organization wouldn't want those attributes? We've learned that vitality is good for stockholders, for customers, and for employees—yet it is unusual in large enterprises.

And that is to their detriment. Whoever masters vitality as a source of performance has an extraordinary competitive edge and provides a deeply satisfying life for themselves and the people they lead.

What We Promise You

As you read through this book, we make three promises to you.

First, we promise a fast-moving, quickly valuable reading experience that features:

- *Principles.* Self-evident rules that provoke new thought and action. While the principles come from what we have observed in our work, they are only valid if they fit with how life works. We trust that an introspective look at your life will serve as proof of the validity of what we say.

- *Examples.* Brief descriptions of the principles in action. We will contrast examples that destroy vitality with those that create it.

- *Practices.* Personal and team activities to test the principles and cultivate your personal and organizational effectiveness.

Second, we promise immediate, positive impact in your life if you read with a specific challenge in mind—your personal *vitality imperative*—that shares these characteristics:

- The challenge is important to you and the organization in which you lead.

- It requires resilient, self-supervising performance from people you lead.

- It requires collaboration across organizational boundaries.

- Success or failure is measurable.

- You are *not* already confident that it will turn out well.

At the end of each chapter, we'll invite you to stop and ask yourself, "What do I now see about my *vitality imperative*, and what action will I take?"

Finally, we promise more days when your leadership feels like an energizing privilege and fewer days it feels like a burden. This promise applies wherever you feel responsible for the success of others: at work, with your family, and in your community.

Of course, our promises only matter if they are relevant to you. So, let's contrast two forms of leadership so that you can decide if *The Vitality Imperative* is worth your time and attention.

Vitality or Not: Different choices for leaders, different experiences for employees

In her foreword, Anne Murray Allen makes the case for vitality. Anne's research fits with our experience over the last thirty years. Energized, committed employees—those who would describe their workplace as exhibiting vitality—create superb, enduring performance. However, creating a Vitality culture is not for the faint of heart and begins with an important choice.

Leaders and philosophers have differed for ages on how to best produce results through others. These can be summed up in two models:

1. *The Superior Leader:* Put superior people in charge and follow their instructions.
2. *The Connected Leader:* Put the most connected people in charge and count on them to understand challenges, inspire commitment, and coordinate contribution.

The Superior Leader Model

The Superior Leader approach is, at best, benevolent domination. Many leaders have produced significant value doing exactly this. The results, however, are rarely sustainable after the organization grows enough to require self-supervising work. There are exceptions, but they tend to feature unusual competitive advantages like a unique technology, market opportunity, or a creatively disruptive business model—and even those eventually deteriorate.

Riccardo Muti, a world-renowned musician and conductor, serves as a good example. Muti is said to have musical perception so refined that his hearing is insured for millions of dollars. Currently, he is the music director of the Chicago Symphony Orchestra and has held important posts in Florence, Philadelphia, Salzburg, London, and Milan. "Muti is brilliant," says a fellow musician. "Not only his instructions are clear, but also the sanction: what will happen if you don't do what he tells you to do. It works to a certain point."

Despite Muti's brilliance, his tenure at Milan's famed Teatro alla Scala, known internationally as La Scala, ended badly. In 2005, nearly all of the seven hundred employees of La Scala signed a letter of no confidence to Muti. The letter said, among other things, "You are using us as instruments, not as partners."

Muti resigned, citing "staff hostility." He contributed to La Scala with years of musical excellence, and yet, he reached the limits of his way of leading. La Scala was ready to move on without him.

The Connected Leader Model

By contrast, the Connected Leader approach largely depends on leaders with unique gifts in the art of connection. These are women and men who intuitively grasp how to connect people to each other and reality in a way that reveals opportunity and inspires high performance. They tend to spearhead times of surprising achievement that leave people feeling proud and deeply satisfied.

Greg Merten, an influential leader at Hewlett-Packard from 1972–2003, is a great example of a Connected Leader. For much of his time at HP, Greg was a senior vice president responsible for Inkjet supplies. He oversaw operations in the United States, Europe, Asia, and Latin America. Greg felt strongly that a large multinational group of employees and supply-chain partners could operate as a community held together by shared purpose, values, and learning. During his tenure, the business results were extraordinary and turnover of high-performing employees was very low. When he retired, the employees of the HP site in Aguadilla, Puerto Rico engraved the following words on a parting gift:

Thanks, Greg:

For caring more than others thought was wise,

For dreaming more than others thought was practical,

For risking more than others thought was safe,

And for expecting more than others thought was possible.

Those are the words of a community of people who felt connected, cared for, and challenged to do great things.

As HP has since shown, you can damage and lose such vitality. Historically, the problem with the Connected Leader model is that it is dependent upon the presence of unusually gifted people. When those people depart, the deterioration of vitality often begins.

With *The Vitality Imperative,* we make connected leadership learnable. The principles and practices serve those who choose the Connected Leader approach to organizational success. It is an important choice between two very different methods of control: the personal brilliance of a few or the connected contribution of many—a choice that can literally change the entire course of an organization.

As one executive told us, "I got to a place in the growth of this company where I needed to change. We had succeeded because a few of us were smart, vigilant, and demanding. That was our era of 'hands-on control.' However, as we got bigger there was a lot of unsupervised work going on and hands-on control was not enough. We've spent the last few years changing how we lead so the company continues to grow. These Vitality principles have helped us enter the era of 'remote control.' It has been uncomfortable, sometimes difficult, and well worth it. We are getting more done with less time, money, and stress."

The Damaging Impact of the Superior Leader Model

We have analyzed thousands of employee surveys across the world and conducted live interviews with employees on six continents. We have discovered that when the Superior Leader approach has outlived its value, the employee experience includes three damaging impacts: fear, mechanics, and manipulation.

1. *Fear* of embarrassment, fear of failure, fear of retribution, and general fear of disappointing someone in a position of power. When people experience fear, they tend to avoid conflict and suppress open dialogue. That lack of candor, as we will discuss later, is a major cause of waste, stress, and mistrust. Criticism and threat feel normal.

2. *Mechanics* are the rule. Rather than feeling supported by processes that make the right thing easy, people report how bureaucratic rules and habits keep them from getting work done. They feel dominated by out-of-date processes and measures that impede contribution. Those processes seem to lack a living spirit because they make employees feel like inanimate objects rather than human beings who want to help.

3. *Manipulation* results in widespread mistrust in the communication coming from leadership. Authenticity feels like the exception, not the norm. Leaders are falsely positive instead of open and honest about the problems facing the company and them personally. Leaders lecture employees about better behavior instead of demonstrating the behavior themselves. The company makes brand promises in marketing campaigns that feel nothing like how it operates day-to-day.

We are not saying that these leaders are committed to fear, mechanics, and manipulation; we are saying that the Superior Leader approach frequently generates these experiences as the enterprise outgrows the personal brilliance of its leaders. If any of your associates are reporting these types of experiences, it is good evidence that Vitality is at risk or already seriously damaged in your organization.

The Positive Impact of the Connected Leader Model

Employees of a Connected Leader organization report very different things than those of a Superior Leader organization. The former group reports a culture of energized high performance, which is *The Vitality Imperative* in action. When asked what explains their energy, commitment, and success, they report three things:

1. *Community* is a sense of belonging, rooted in common values and common purpose— the experience of being "in this together," and looking out for one another on the journey to a shared achievement. In a genuine high-performance community, our differences combined with trust produce brilliance. Whereas most leaders only think about trust when it is at risk, Vitality leaders create trust ahead of time so there is always more trust in the relational bank when they need to make a withdrawal.

2. *Contribution* means making a meaningful difference. The enjoyment of contribution is deeply human. Have you ever stopped in the middle of mowing a lawn and admired the difference between the short grass and the long grass? We all love being valuable and leaving things better than we found them. When vitality is the norm, people report feeling like the solution rather than the problem. They feel recognized for their contributions and believe that their leaders work to make the right thing easy and the wrong thing hard in support of those contributions.

3. *Choice* is the victory of commitment over compliance. Each of us chooses to be devoted or not; it cannot be demanded. When vitality is present, people report thoroughly understanding strategy and priorities and personally choose to support success. They report a personal relationship to organizational values and adopt them as their own. This deep clarity and ownership lead to more decision-making discretion. Colleagues feel trusted, and it takes less time to get things done. Connected leaders have the awareness and skill needed to inspire committed choice rather than merely demand compliance.

Vital organizations reliably achieve more with less time, money, and stress. When that energized performance is present, people report experiences of community, contribution, and choice.

Betting on vitality, however, requires different awareness and skill than betting on personal brilliance and position power. For the last twenty-five years, we have appreciated that awareness and skill in leaders around the world, and we now know this: there is a design to vitality, and a committed leader can learn the design and put it to work—both personally and organizationally.

Fanning the Flame of Vitality

Eons ago, humans valued fire and yet could not create it. When lightning struck (literally), people captured the fire and tended to it carefully to keep it available for warmth, protection, and cooking. Keepers of the flame sustained the precious resource. When the fire went out, it was gone until lightning struck again. Eventually, we learned to create fire, not just catch it, and the human experience was transformed.

Vitality is a bit like that. Most leaders are grateful when it strikes but are not all that great at conjuring it at will. From our research into vitality, leaders who reliably create and fan the flame of vitality have organized their awareness and skills into seven promises that are divided into two categories: igniting vitality and sustaining it over time.

In our experience, the defining difference between those who employ the Superior Leader model and those who champion the Connected Leader model is the willingness to engage with and keep these seven vital promises.

Igniting the Fire

Igniting the fire of vitality takes creating the right conditions. Just as you can't start a fire in the rain without the proper spark or without combustible materials, you cannot create vitality in an organization without inviting connection. This takes intention and commitment. In our experience, there are four key elements that create an environment conducive to igniting vitality:

1. **Presence: Awareness without prejudice**
   Presence is to vitality what oxygen is to fire. Each of the other promises depends on the quality of presence. So, cultivating presence is a crucial act of leadership.

2. **Empathy: The power to appreciate the purposes, worries, and circumstances of others**
   Leadership without empathy is ill-informed at best and bullying at worst. Empathy is not "soft." It is courageous, skillful, and wise to quickly comprehend the world of another and all influence depends on it.

3. **Purpose: The mutual resolve of a community**
   Authentic purpose lowers supervision costs while improving performance. It is not only logical, but felt emotionally and physically. We will share ways to locate the intersection between the deep personal purposes of individuals and the important purposes of an enterprise.

4. **Authenticity: Accelerating achievement through truth**
   Living true to ourselves and to our word sounds right and yet doing so can be a major challenge. Authenticity, however, is not just a moral imperative, it is also a skill. We will explore how a well-told truth creates connection and turns conflict into useful intelligence.

Sustaining the Fire

Igniting vitality in an organization is not enough, however. If not sustained, cared for, and fed, vitality will eventually blow out. In our experience, there are three more promises that must be kept to sustain vitality in an organization once it has been ignited:

5. **Wonder: Fueling the fire and keeping our best day in front of us**
   Creativity and innovation rest on wonder. In this book, we will show how practices that combine curiosity and possibility free us from imaginary limits and inspire fresh thinking.

6. **Timing: The victory of evolution over revolution**
   Revolution is an act of desperation for people who have been bad at evolution. When we are good at seeing and acting on what it is time for, we create less resistance and more cooperation. We will share what we have learned about timing and how it builds organizational agility.

7. **Surprising Results: Making a meaningful, continual, and energizing difference**
   Vitality grows in cycles of surprise. When people produce valuable results beyond their own expectations, there is widespread, energizing delight. The key is designing and delivering short cycles of surprise, and we will show you how.

This book will explore each of these promises and show how, together, those promises ignite and sustain community, contribution, and choice. The image below summarizes our offer. If it is attractive to you, then we welcome you as a fellow traveler and ask that you read on.

Throughout the book, we will invite you to visit ***thevitalityimperative.com***, an online resource intended to be a "reader's companion" that supports and deepens your exploration of these ideas.

PROMISE #1

PRESENCE:

Awareness without Prejudice

It is easy to miss valuable "weak signals" often hidden amid the noise.
—*McKinsey Quarterly*

The greatest gift you can give another is the purity of your attention.
—Richard Moss

*We cannot change what we are not aware of, and once we are aware,
we cannot help but change.*
—Sheryl Sandberg, COO Facebook

In 1986, a 14-year-old violinist named Midori Goto, known simply by
her first name, performed Leonard Bernstein's Serenade in her debut
with the Boston Symphony Orchestra at the Tanglewood music festival.
As Bernstein himself conducted this challenging piece, the E string on
Midori's violin snapped. She turned gracefully to the concertmaster, took
his violin, and resumed her play. Moments later, the same string snapped
on the replacement violin, and again she turned to the concertmaster, took
yet another violin, and returned seamlessly to the performance.

In spite of the disruptions, *The New York Times'* John Rockwell termed
Midori's performance "near perfect." When the piece ended, amid wild
cheers and applause, Bernstein knelt and kissed her hand in honor of her
poise and musicianship. Her capacity to be present amid the mayhem was

remarkable. We think every one of us can learn to be as poised as Midori through the power of presence.

How Does Presence Produce "More with Less"?

Presence is as crucial to vitality as oxygen is to fire.

Presence dictates how much of our mental, emotional, and physical talents are available to us at a given moment. Many leaders tell us about precious days when they were especially perceptive and effective, operating at the top of their talents. If you want to spend a greater percentage of life experiencing those kinds of days, then get very interested in presence.

By presence we do not mean charisma; we mean awareness. How well leaders are connected to a given moment governs their impact per unit of time, money, and stress. More fully, presence is the ability to be aware intellectually, emotionally, and physically without prejudice—that is, any preconception that pollutes our awareness. There are big stakes here because both insight and action are correlated to awareness. If you miss the moment, you'll miss the signals crucial to your success. The quality of your future is directly correlated with the quality of your presence.

Practicing presence is not common. Common practices and wise ones, however, can be different, and quite often are. In our conversations with people around the world, we hear that there is "not enough time" for such new pursuits. Typical solutions to the not-enough-time dilemma often make things worse. We hurry, multitask, and give shallow attention to each moment as we rush toward the next one. Meeting agendas feature many subjects, but few things are resolved.

The outcome? Maximum effort and minimum impact. As a result, impatience increases and effectiveness declines, leaving even more to be done.

We think it is time for the victory of presence over this irrational cycle of waste.

The victory of presence has major benefits to community, contribution, and choice:

- Increased trust
- Better judgment and decision making

- Noticing "weak signals" that others miss
- Greater safety, fewer injuries
- Greater peace of mind and enjoyment of work

If you care about those benefits, then there is good news: presence is improvable.

A leader's ability to make a meaningful difference rises and falls with the quality of presence. In this chapter, we will cover the principles of presence, introduce some basic practices to develop presence, and show you how to recover presence when it is lost. Let's investigate.

Presence Principle #1: Presence is rational, emotional, and physical

All humans think, feel, and act. Noticing that triad of human experience is essential to presence.

Daniel Goleman, in *Vital Lies, Simple Truths*, wrote, "The range of what we think and do is limited by what we fail to notice." If you want to strengthen presence, start by noticing thoughts, emotions, and body movement. Notice your own experience, and notice others'. This deceptively simple practice of awareness improves insight and action, while lack of awareness assures that you are not fully connected to yourself or to others—dangerous territory for a leader.

We sponsor an executive development program called "Credibility, Influence, and Impact." Leaders from organizations around the world participate, and most report that the work on presence is one of the most valuable parts of the experience. Here is what two of them have to say.

Roger Henderson was a successful senior engineering manager at Ball Aerospace when his career took a turn. Roger's interest in the design principles underlying human performance led him to become a director of talent development and a valued coach for senior executives at Ball. He says:

I now see the mental, emotional, and physical components of presence as fundamental to personnel development. These three pinpoint precise aspects of the human experience and allow for focused attention. Leaving even one of these areas unattended hampers growth. The development process accelerates simply by having people go from unaware to aware in all three areas. We discover thoughts, moods, and physical habits that impede progress. We easily identify useful actions to take because an aware leader sees things an unaware leader cannot. Many of the people I coach are very talented, very successful, and all it takes is an increase in this triple awareness for performance to improve.

An executive in charge of corporate affairs in a Fortune Global 500 company told us what he thinks about the three parts of presence:

Working from the components of presence has changed how we manage media relations, investor relations, all internal and external communication. We were unaware of how unbalanced our approach was—mainly intellectual and very little emotional and physical. No wonder we got unsatisfactory results: we were only connecting to one-third of how people receive a communication. We still make sure the logic is clear. Now, we also research the emotions important to us and our audience, plus the impact on the physical circumstances in which people live and work. When we weave all that in, our communication is less formal, more human, and produces more of the results we want.

To echo Daniel Goleman, if you notice what you previously failed to notice, you will think and do things you could never do before. When you notice thoughts, emotions, and physical activity, you start the presence improvement journey.

Presence Principle #2: The first act of leadership is presence

Presence is where leadership begins. The present is the *only* place we envision the future, learn from the past, and cause progress. When our presence is compromised, so is our leadership.

"Back when I did not have a senior executive position, I found out that many people thought of me as introverted. Since I became CEO that now is interpreted as aloof," one CEO told us. "Also, before people thought of me as someone who asked challenging questions. Now I hear that I'm intimidating. I know my ability to lead is damaged if people think I'm aloof and intimidating."

Near the launch of his tenure, our friend made a simple change to fix this perception: whenever he's in the elevator or moving through the office, he puts his smartphone away and greets anyone he sees.

"Really being with people is something I've had to cultivate because it is more comfortable and automatic for me to be with the smartphone and answer a few messages," he said. "The results have been encouraging. I hear that people actually think of me as a colleague who cares about who they are, not just what they do. Also, people open up more and tell me things I did not know—very useful."

When someone is headfirst in their smartphone, answering a text, or otherwise distracted while you're speaking to them, what thoughts do you have? How do you feel? How does your body react?

Now, compare your reactions to a time when someone was devoted to and focused on understanding you. What were your thoughts, emotions, and physical sensations?

This reveals a simple truth: When you are fully present in a conversation, people feel honored by your attention, relationships are strengthened, and candor is increased. The faith people have in your judgment improves, too.

Much is written about trust in organizations. To build trust, start by giving someone your wholehearted, undivided attention. Pick someone today, and give it a try. Make being fully present in this moment your first act of leadership.

Presence Principle #3: All improvement begins with what is present

An executive in the restaurant business once told us, "You know how you can waste a lot of food? Just add ingredients to a dish without knowing what is already in it."

If you want to improve a strategy, a process, or any kind of performance, first understand how the work is currently done. You will discover that it rarely, if ever, fits your preconceptions. Be present, be curious, and be ready for surprise. Whatever you do, don't try to fix the dish until you know what is in it.

Jim Reinhart is the chief operating officer at QTS, a fast-growing, world-class leader in data center management. We first experienced Jim's commitment to starting with what is present when he was an executive at Capital One sponsoring supply-chain improvements involving internal and supplier processes. When Jim announced workshops to map out how the supply chain was already functioning, many thought that was a waste of time.

Jim heard the fears and criticisms and made a simple request: "Let's try one workshop and see what we get. We need unprecedented results, so I think we need to try something unprecedented. If we get no value, we will rethink the approach." Jim's credibility was sufficient for the many skeptics to give it a try.

In that first workshop, a group representing the whole supply chain, many of whom compete with one another, convened to map out how the work gets done. Reinhart did not want to "fix the dish" until everyone understood what was in it already. The only assignment was to carefully document the process of work entering the system and moving to successful execution. This was the first time all these citizens of the Capital One system were present simultaneously, and they got to see the work through each other's eyes.

As everyone became mutually aware of how the work was done, the workshop facilitators asked people to report what they saw, how they felt, and what they thought about the emerging picture. They were coached to listen, learn, and let go of prejudice.

One of the people who originally doubted the value of the workshop said, "I was surprised by how open and honest people became and how much people cared about their work. We never had those kinds of conversations, and we never had results like that either."

Defensiveness disappeared, and people came together to get more done with less.

According to Reinhart, the workshops initially produced more than $200 million in improvements and the highly present, highly collaborative approach ultimately led to over $1 billion in savings.

Curious presence is an antidote to bias. We have observed huge, negative impact on profit and loss statements, balance sheets, and cash flows when senior executives operate out of prefabricated biases. Leaders who do not begin by understanding what is present waste time, talent, and money by chasing assumptions. Even successful companies like HP, Toyota, and Xerox have experienced billions of dollars of losses when executives failed to appreciate what was present in their own company and the marketplace before pursuing their own preferred acquisition or high-risk investment.

Reinhart's experience shows that Connected Leaders begin with what is present and end up more informed, trusted, and productive. Superior Leaders, on the other hand, tend to think they already know all they need to know. Which leader do you want to be?

Presence Principle #4: Presence improves performance

If we are aware of what is actually happening around us, we naturally operate at the top of our talent. We notice things others miss and take actions others do not. Savvy leaders can help people be more effective by developing better presence.

To make the point, here is a presence experiment we adapted from W. Timothy Gallwey's creative work in *The Inner Game of Golf,* which is illuminating even if you do not play golf.

Get a putter and three golf balls, and position yourself 10 to 15 feet from a golf hole or a similarly sized target (e.g., business card or a drinking glass on its side). You can do this inside on a rug or carpet. Position the ball, and then follow these steps:

1. Notice thoughts you have about putting the ball into the hole. If you are with a trusted friend tell them the thoughts, such as, "I don't have good hand-eye coordination," or "What will this prove?" If alone, just acknowledge those thoughts to yourself. Then take three deep breaths, noticing the moment when you pass from inhale to exhale.

2. Notice emotions that are present, like, "This is embarrassing," or "I feel foolish." Take three deep breaths, noticing the moment when you pass from inhale to exhale.

3. Place your putter behind the ball so you are ready to putt. Close your eyes and putt the ball toward the hole. Then, with eyes closed, predict where the ball went relative to the hole. For example, "I think it is short of the hole by about three feet and to the right about two feet." Open your eyes and notice where it actually went.

4. Close your eyes and hit again. Feel the ball as it touches the face of the putter. Predict where it went. Open eyes and check.

5. Take a deep breath, noticing the passage of your breath from in to out. Close your eyes, hit again, and predict the result.

6. Now, just hit a few putts with your eyes open.

All you did is notice your own thoughts, emotions, and physical sensations. What do you notice about the results? Most people find their predictions get more accurate, and so does their putting. This reveals an essential truth: when you notice other people's thoughts, feelings, and actions, you will find your predictions about them are more accurate, too.

The more we are present, the more naturally our thoughts, emotions, and bodies align with our goals. Effort declines and effectiveness improves. This applies to a lot more than golf. No matter what the subject, presence is key to operating at the top of your talent.

Presence Principle #5: Presence improves with practice

Practicing presence develops our capacity to give our attention rather than have it taken, and cultivating presence produces practical results. The following passage is from the February 15, 2010 edition of *Penn News*. The article uses "mindfulness" for much of what we mean by "presence."

A University of Pennsylvania-led study in which training was provided to a high-stress U.S. military group preparing for deployment to Iraq has demonstrated a positive link between mindfulness training, or MT, and improvements in mood and working memory. Mindfulness is the ability to be aware and attentive of the present moment without emotional reactivity or volatility.

The study found that the more time participants spent engaging in daily mindfulness exercises, the better their mood, working memory (the cognitive term for complex thought), problem solving, and cognitive control of emotions. The study also suggested that sufficient mindfulness training may protect against functional impairments associated with high-stress challenges that require a tremendous amount of cognitive control, self-awareness, situational awareness, and emotional regulation—something leaders in all complex organizations face.

Presence is not a "soft skill"—it is a hard business asset and worthy of practice. And everyone who relies on your judgment benefits when you strengthen your presence.

Practicing Presence: What you can do to improve

We've covered a lot of ideas on the power of presence. If there's one thing we've learned from our time working with busy executives, it's that we're quicker to understand ideas than to take action on them. These practices are designed to turn ideas into action.

Knowledge is powerful, but it is not transformative until it is put into practice. At the end of each chapter we will share three to four practices we know improve connected leadership. These practices are designed to help you apply the knowledge you gain so that you can achieve the results you want with less time, money, and stress. Think of them as investments.

When it comes to presence, we suggest you practice in all three areas:

- *Physical:* presence of body
- *Emotional:* presence of emotion
- *Rational:* presence of mind

Presence cannot be forced and occurs most naturally through a mood of relaxed vigilance.

To demonstrate, here is a quick experiment. Put a coin on a table. Tense the muscles in your forearms and hands and, with the muscles still tense, pick up the coin. Then, consciously relax your forearms and hands, and pick up the coin.

What do you notice?

Most people report they pick up the coin more easily and quickly the second time. Tension also can be mental (worry) and emotional (anxiety). The first practice is simply relaxing our body, emotions, and mind so that we can more easily pick up what is happening around us physically, emotionally, and mentally.

Now, let's add vigilance. To be vigilant is to be consciously attentive. Have someone toss you five or six colored markers at the same time. What happened? Now, ask the person to pick up the markers and prepare to toss them to you again. This time, however, focus all your attention on one marker, as though catching it earns you $1 million. Take a breath, relax, and smile as they're tossed. What happened?

If you easily and calmly caught the one marker, even as the other ones flew at you, you experienced the special benefit of relaxed vigilance. Relaxed vigilance takes conscious practice, which you can do throughout the day. The goal of the practice is to:

- *Notice* tension.
- *Breathe* consciously.
- *Relax* your muscles, mind, and emotions.
- *Focus* your attention (give attention rather than have it taken).

You can easily practice that flow in taking the actions we suggest next.

Presence Practice #1: Physical awareness

Physical practices are a convenient fast track to improving presence. While our minds may wander, our body is always right here.

Physical Practice: Move it!

Years ago we met someone who used to work directly with Walt Disney. He told us that whenever creative thinking was needed and missing, Walt would say, "Change the setting!" People would get up and move—maybe go for a walk, find another place to meet, or simply get up and change the configuration of the furniture in the room. Most of the time, new thinking emerged in the new setting.

Movement tends to awaken all our senses, increase presence, and energize thinking. A few suggestions:

- Have a walking meeting. Grab a notebook or note cards in case someone says something brilliant.

- In the same vein, the next time your own thinking gets stuck, go for a walk. Notice how heavily your feet hit the ground; see if you can step more lightly, then even more lightly. Then, add force to your step and notice the heaviness increase. Then, just enjoy the walk.

- If you are working at your desk, stand up every twenty minutes to stretch, take a few steps, look out a window, and notice something new.

Your *Vitality Imperative*

Earlier, we asked you to keep a real *vitality imperative* in mind as you move through the book. Think of that challenge now. What aspects of it cause you tension? Where is your body taut?

Now, take a deep breath, and as you exhale relax the points of tension in your body.

Any worries? Notice them, breathe, and relax.

Any stressful emotions? Notice them, breathe, and relax.

For you, what is most important about your imperative? Give your attention to that thought and read on.

- If you are having a bad day, hike up a moderate hill. It is hard to stay negative during a pleasant uphill walk. Start up the incline and position your body like you are dismayed, fatigued, or beaten (e.g., slumped shoulders). Then, shift to a posture of confidence (e.g., back straight, chest up and out, chin level to the ground). Do both again. Stay with the one you like.

- Do a performance review in an unexpected setting. Ask the other person where he or she would like to go. Go there and have the conversation.

- In general, move frequently while you notice breathing, posture, and details of your environment.

Movement restores the connection between mind, emotion, and body. In his book *Get Up!*, Dr. James Levine says, "Sitting is the new smoking." Levine maintains that sitting all day is unnatural and to blame for all kinds of ailments. "This is about hard-core productivity. You will make money if your workforce gets up and gets moving. Your kids will get better grades if they get up and get moving," he says. "The science is not refuted."

Presence Practice #2: Emotional awareness

To have emotions is to be human. Some people diminish emotion and instead worship logic, which is a big mistake if you work with human beings. Emotions are an animating force that motivate us to decide and act. Brilliant researchers like Dan Lovallo, Nina Mažar, and Dan Ariely have shown that big decisions in companies and personal lives have rich emotional elements. As Ariely says, we are "predictably irrational."

While some discount emotion, others seem ruled by emotion. Neither extreme leads to organizational Vitality, which, if you recall, is achieving more with less time, money, and stress. When a Vitality leader can wisely honor emotion and not be victimized by it, we call that emotional agility.

Most of us are not skilled at naming or expressing our feelings. Rather, we default to talking about our feelings instead of acting from them with confidence. In the process, we lose the clarity and choice regarding the emotions that animate our actions.

So, for instance, one might say, "I feel that you should have included me in the decision," rather than, "I felt hurt and insignificant when I was not included in the decision." The former is a thought; the latter is emotion.

Knowing how you feel is essential for powerful communication. If you learn to distinguish a rich palette of feelings and express them consciously, you will upgrade your own intelligence and the influence you have on others.

Emotional Practice: Name it

The following is a set of six common emotional "families." Each family is defined by words that describe the emotion on a continuum from moderate to intense:

- *Glad:* from approval to elation
- *Sad:* from disappointment to despair
- *Mad:* from disapproval to fury
- *Afraid:* from avoidance to terror
- *Ashamed:* from embarrassed to guilty
- *Content:* from relaxed to serene

Our promise: if you do the 5-minute process below once a day for three weeks, you will dramatically improve your emotional awareness and agility, and people will notice.

1. Name a significant event or experience that happened that day. Anything that the word "significant" brings to mind will work.

2. Scan the emotional families and pick the one that best describes your most prominent emotions regarding the event or experience.

3. Using a 1-10 scale, how moderate or extreme is the emotion? What word or words describe that spot on the continuum?

4. What happened that triggered the emotion?

5. What is most important to you about the situation? What other emotions arise when you consider what is most important to you?

Emotional Families Scale

Glad

approval 1 2 3 4 5 6 7 8 9 10 elation

Sad

disappointment 1 2 3 4 5 6 7 8 9 10 despair

Mad

disapproval 1 2 3 4 5 6 7 8 9 10 fury

Afraid

avoidance 1 2 3 4 5 6 7 8 9 10 terror

Ashamed

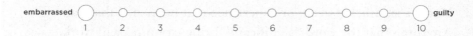

embarrassed 1 2 3 4 5 6 7 8 9 10 guilty

Content

relaxed 1 2 3 4 5 6 7 8 9 10 serene

6. Of all the emotions that could be triggered by the event, which increase your vitality? Which decrease your vitality?

7. Breathe deeply and relax.

When we name and are present to our experience, we are in the position to compare and choose emotion, which is vital to emotional agility. The more you practice, the better you will get at aligning emotion with your most important purposes.

Presence Practice #3: Rational awareness

The great poet John Milton wrote in *Paradise Lost,* "The mind is its own place, and in itself / Can make a Heaven of Hell, a Hell of Heaven."

Our minds are active, attempting to make sense of our world. The sense-making work we do can either help or hurt our most important purposes. The more aware we are, the more we have presence of mind.

There are many practices for improving presence of mind. What follows are a tried-and-true few.

Mental Practice: Be for, not against

Most people move through congested areas with their attention on what is in the way. The next time you are in a crowded airport, train station, or shopping mall, focus your mind on a simple thought: "Where are the open spaces?" You will find yourself easily slipping into them.

This simple exercise illustrates the power of focusing on what you are for (open spaces) versus what you are against (people in your way). If we focus only on what we are against, survivalist emotions dominate as we give our attention to what we don't want versus what we do. Tension rises and mental agility declines. In the presence of what we are for, our minds are fully engaged, relaxed vigilance is easier, tension goes down, and our mental agility goes up.

In an agile mind, what we are against simply informs what we are for rather than distracts from it. For instance, the people in our way in a crowd serve to help us see open spaces rather than present themselves as obstacles.

Your *Vitality Imperative*

Bring to mind the challenge you are using to assess the value of vitality. Make two quick lists:

- What are you for? What values, purposes, results, or opportunities are on your mind?

- What are you against? What criticisms, concerns, impediments, or risks are on your mind?

Then, looking at your "against" list, ask yourself, "What am I for that has me be against that?" If new things come to mind, add to the "for" list. Next:

- Give your relaxed, vigilant interest to each entry on the "for" list. What ideas or actions come to mind?

- Give your relaxed, vigilant interest to the entries on the "against" list. How many of them have been addressed already by focusing on what you are for? What additional ideas or actions come to mind?

Vitality Is Increased When Presence Is Practiced

Practicing presence—and actually getting better at it—is unusual. Those who make the practice habitual have an unusually clear and accurate connection to what is happening, unusual poise under pressure, and better access to their own talents. Also, presence is infectious. Your calm interest in what is actually happening can relax others and make a whole group smarter. In *Social Intelligence,* Goleman said, "We catch each other's mood like we catch a cold." The mood of presence is worth catching.

Here are some questions worth considering as you decide whether or not you want to promise presence in your personal and professional life:

- Where and when is it important for me to be fully present?
- How does the quality of my presence help or hurt the connections that build *community*?
- How does my presence help or hurt people making a significant *contribution*?
- How does my presence influence people making a *choice* to do great work?
- How can I develop more presence today? What, if anything, will I do differently?

To advance your mastery of presence, more resources and practices—including those referenced throughout the chapter—can be found at ***thevitalityimperative.com/presence***.

When it comes to being a Vitality leader, presence is the first thing. However, it is not everything, so let's move on!

PROMISE #2

EMPATHY:

The Power to Appreciate the Purposes, Worries, and Circumstances of Others

You never really understand a person until you consider things from his point of view—until you climb into his skin and walk around in it.

—Harper Lee, *To Kill a Mockingbird*

People believe leaders who really understand and care about their aspirations and struggles. And when people believe in their leaders, everything is easier.

—Al Miksch, CEO, Audio Precision

Every year, more than 20 million babies are born prematurely and at risk of dying. Of those premature births that do result in death, 98 percent occur in the developing world in large part because the infants cannot be kept warm.

Stanford's design institute, known as the d.school, features a curriculum that teaches empathy as fundamental to great design. In 2007, a group of d.school students took on a formidable challenge: design a solution to neonatal hypothermia that costs less than one percent of a state-of-the-art incubator.

The students began by listening to learn the purposes, worries, and circumstances of the parents in developing regions. While visiting rural India, they discovered that many incubators went unused because the hospitals were too far from the villages. Also, midwives delivered most children at home, while hospitals were strange and feared. Even if incubators could be made more cheaply and brought to the villages, unreliable electricity was a prohibitive problem. Devoted mothers were worried about keeping their babies warm in circumstances that precluded traditional incubator solutions.

This empathetic research led to crucial criteria: any solution needed to be locally available, nonelectrical, portable, sterile, and reusable. During the discovery process, parents, midwives, and doctors at local clinics felt understood and respected, and they in turn became creative co-conspirators.

The result was an extraordinary, elegant solution that looks much like a tiny sleeping bag. Using waterproof materials like those in high-tech camping gear, the students made a hooded wrap to fully enclose the baby. An insulated sleeve in the back of the hooded wrap holds a wax-like material that can be heated in water and hold the resulting temperature for four to six hours. Close to one hundred fifty thousand babies have benefited from the solution, a product known as Embrace.

This story serves to illustrate what we've learned from our work with four hundred organizations in more than one hundred countries:

- People long to be understood. When you appreciate *purposes, worries,* and *circumstances,* people feel known.
- People long to be valued. When you learn from others, they feel valuable and legitimatized.
- Connecting with those deep longings unlocks contribution and causes vitality to soar.

The Economist honored the Embrace cofounders as winners of the 2013 Innovation award for social and economic innovation. Such is the power of honoring the innately human desire to be heard and valuable. True innovation begins not with assumptions and opinions; instead, it begins with deep, empathetic research that creates communities of contribution.

Imagine what putting this type of innovative empathy to work in your organization could achieve. What amazing things could happen?

How Does Empathy Produce More with Less?

The Vitality Imperative is rooted in a single principle: to align leadership practices with human nature. People are not things. They are not mechanical elements in a business process. Every time we forget that, we add time, money, and stress to work. Empathy is fundamental to our nature and yet woefully under emphasized in leadership development.

To be human is to empathize. It is the reason we care about love *and* war, family *and* work, collaboration *and* competition. A great Vitality leader connects to all that, and uses skillful, proactive empathy to quickly and correctly connect with another. How important is that quick and correct ability to comprehend the perspectives of others? As we shall see, it is imperative for any leader who wants greater results.

What Empathy Is Not

Many would consider empathy "soft." We know a successful hostage team leader who would adamantly disagree.

"'Soft'? That's ridiculous," he says. "If you want to resolve a hostage incident without bloodshed, you better be good at getting in someone else's skin. When you can think their thoughts and feel what they are feeling, you can anticipate what they'll do. And when you really 'get' what it is going on for them, a lot of the time they start talking and that increases the chances of finding a solution. All negotiators without empathy can do is try to get people in front of a window for a clear shot."

This goes to show that empathy is not pity, not condescending, and is definitely not "soft." Leaders lacking in empathy are ill-informed at best and bullies at worst. Without empathy, we resort to manipulation and spin, and squander the chance for real inspiration. The result is often a lot of organizational bloodshed.

Conversely, the tangible benefits of empathy to community, contribution, and choice are:

- *Empathy improves relationships and accountability* and, in turn, lowers supervision costs.
- *Empathy accelerates learning.*

- *Empathy is the antidote to prejudice.* Sexism, racism, and thoughtless prejudice of all kinds decline as empathy increases.

- *Empathy increases candor.* As understanding increases, so does disclosure.

- *Empathy reduces mistrust and increases influence.*

- *Empathy improves anticipation.* The more empathetic you are, the more you can predict the behavior of others.

Now, let's look at how empathy works and how we can improve.

The Human Need for Empathy

Our brains contain two basic drives crucial to our evolution: to survive and to socialize.

Our drive to survive prioritizes safety, responding to threats within three seconds by fighting, fleeing, freezing, or appeasing. It is based in visceral, individualistic self-interest. Our deep longing for survival is the source of much conflict and destruction in the world, and often manifests itself in aggression, of which the brilliant physicist Stephen Hawking said, "The human failing I would most like to correct is aggression. It may have had survival advantage in caveman days, to get more food, territory, or a partner with whom to reproduce, but now it threatens to destroy us all."

Our drive to socialize, on the other hand, prioritizes connection, surfacing deeply embedded desires to affiliate, belong, and cooperate. It is based on being safer, smarter, and stronger together than we are separately. Our deep longing to socialize is the source of teamwork and crucial to human resilience and achievement. Empathy—which, conversely, Hawking said he would like to see most magnified in humanity—unlocks the power of our drive to socialize.

In the introductory chapter, we said that vitality-destroying leadership features fear, mechanics, and manipulation. In our work around the world, we have discovered that such conditions exist when leaders act from the drive to survive more than the drive to socialize. To cultivate vitality, leaders must strengthen their capacity for empathy, which increases community, contribution, and choice.

Let's explore the principles and techniques that make empathy a readily available leadership asset.

Empathy Principle #1: The test for listening is learning

In the 2014 *Financial Times* article "The Quiet Art of Being a Good Listener," Jeff Immelt, General Electric's chief executive, is quoted as saying that listening is "the single most undervalued and underdeveloped business skill." Just as important, however, is the quality of our listening. Too many people think the test for listening is repeating back words we hear. And too often we listen to confirm our biases rather than to learn things that might challenge them and lead to greater organizational health and wealth.

In the same article, author Alicia Clegg shares the story of how Intuit's founder Scott Cook missed out on four years of major profits by listening with confirmation bias rather than to learn.

> *Mr. Cook recalls being baffled by a survey that suggested Intuit's customers were using Quicken, its money-management software, for business accounting even though it was designed for ordinary consumers. The finding seemed absurd, so he ignored it, reasoning that respondents meant they used Quicken to sort out their personal finances during office breaks. But when Intuit delved deeper—some four years later—it transpired that small businesses were indeed buying the product because, unlike professional software, it did not assume knowledge of debit and credit accounting. The discovery led to the development of QuickBooks, now Intuit's biggest revenue generator. "Such is our tendency to find explanations that conform to our beliefs that we'll often persist in [error] rather than accept data that confronts [our preconceptions]," he says. Mr. Cook had been guilty of "confirmation bias."*

Over the last thirty years, we have discovered that the antidote to confirmation bias is listening to learn. The challenge is formidable. Most people are curious as a thoughtless reaction. Empathetic leaders, however, are curious as a promise. If you can generate intentional curiosity, you can listen to learn in three fast-moving stages: recognize, respect and discover, and intersect.

1. Recognize

Learn what people are for (purposes), what people are against (worries), and the facts of the situation (circumstances). Get good at learning these three things and you will connect more quickly and deeply than most people.

The first step is simply to recognize, not to agree or disagree. If you want to make sense of someone's behavior, first recognize what they are for, against, and the facts commanding their attention, and let everything else (mood, personality, etc.) fade into the unimportant background.

This, of course, takes presence. Relax, breathe, and give yourself fully to hearing their purposes, worries, and circumstances. You will tap into the other person's deep longing to be understood.

2. Respect and Discover

What, from the other person's perspective, is legitimate about their purposes, worries, and circumstances? Are you willing to be surprised by their point of view? Are you willing to discover their contribution? If yes, you will tap into that person's deep longing to be respected and valued.

Typically, the moment you do something I disagree with, I begin to criticize. I quickly list your shortcomings and ascribe multiple bad motivations like ignorance, ineptitude, revenge, greed, or jealousy. It takes courage and discipline to stop, take a breath, and wonder things like, "How would she explain her behavior? What in her is worthy of my respect?" Can you set aside irrational, rapid opinions about the other, research legitimacy, and be ready for surprise?

This takes putting aside our confirmation biases in order to enhance our capacity for surprising discovery, much like Cook's discovery of the need for a small-business accounting suite.

3. Intersect

Reveal mutual interest and common ground. Listening is like radar. When you focus your listening on a question like, "What can I learn?" an extraordinary thing happens: your radar starts to collect information, insights, and lessons that would otherwise go unnoticed. The moment you learn something new, you've left the confines of your own viewpoint—and that is essential to empathy. You begin to notice, however small, common ground where your and another's point of view overlap. We call that spot the intersection.

The intersection has three vectors: my view, your view, and the facts that affect us both.

Finding where our interests intersect is a product of empathy, and it reveals a lot. If I treat your view as legitimate as mine, then I can genuinely ask, "Where do we agree? What do we have to give one another? What possibility lives at the intersection?" Even though many disagreements may remain, a point of intersection can launch collaboration, creating a new foundation of trust that helps to resolve other differences.

This takes a commitment to focusing on where we agree. A major mistake we see in negotiations is starting meetings with a list of disagreements. That triggers defensiveness and makes resolution hard and long. If you want to move quickly, first find common ground, and then address disagreement.

Empathy Principle #2: Where you get resistance, do research

Some years ago, one of us represented a client in the attempted purchase of a privately held company. After a rigorous, independent valuation, our client made what he thought was a fair offer. Not only was the offer rejected, but it was countered with a price 30 percent higher than the valuation. Our client's first reaction was to threaten to walk away from the deal without further discussion, hoping that move would bring the owner of the business "to his senses." It did not. The man still held out for his high price.

We decided this resistance merited research, and after curious and respectful conversation, we discovered the following about the potential seller's point of view:

- *Purpose:* He wanted to deepen the stature and respect he had with fellow members of the business community where he lived.

- *Worry:* If he did not sell for a higher price than a similar business sold, he would look weak and taken advantage of.

- *Circumstance:* He was retiring at the end of an active career, and he wanted to spend his time playing golf with people he wanted to impress.

Once the seller felt understood and respected, he admitted that his valuation was above market. All he wanted was the top line to meet his number. He offered to personally assume some of the company debt to offset the higher valuation. Our client agreed, and the deal went through. We are confident that if our client just kept telling the seller his valuation was crazy, the deal would have never closed.

Can you think of the last time someone resisted your well-intended contribution? When that happened, what did you think, feel, and do?

Many people simply get more passionate, make the same point again, and try to show the flaws in the other's point of view. That is a mistake. In fact, if you want to make sure someone does *not* get your point, tell him or her they are wrong, and then try and make your case again. When resistance is strong ("I'm right, and they are wrong"), it looks like this:

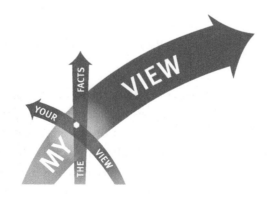

From the last thirty years of trial, error, and success, we have come to believe that people only resist you because of a perceived threat to a deeply held purpose, worry, and/or circumstance. If you try to dominate, resistance increases. If you do not remove that sense of danger, they cannot hear your true intent. Removing the danger requires reflection and preparation. Such was the case with our client purchasing that business.

On the following page is the Presence-Empathy Deep Dive that we often use with our clients to help sort through thorny conflicts. If you are experiencing resistance about something important, it will be worth your while to fill it out.

A Presence-Empathy Deep Dive: Keeping the empathy promise

PRESENCE	Thoughts	Emotions	Actions	Themes
Purposes (for)				
Worries (against)				
Circumstances (facts)				

©2015 Conversant

Here are a few tips:
1. Respectfully name the subject that is causing resistance.
   To be respectful, the other party should recognize the subject
   and not be insulted by how you describe the issue.
2. Fill out a Presence-Empathy Deep Dive for yourself first.
   a. Purpose
      What are you for?
      What positive emotions are present?
      What actions are you taking?
   b. Worries
      What are you against?
      What negative emotions are present?
      What actions are you taking?
   c. Circumstances
      What do you think are the most important facts?
      How do you feel about those facts?
      What are you currently doing about those facts?
   d. In the far right column, discover and note themes across your
      purposes, worries, and circumstances.
   e. Fill out a deep dive for the other person. There are three ways
      to do this.

      If you are very familiar with their point of view then trust that
      and, using their words whenever possible, fill it out.

      If you are unfamiliar but know someone who is very familiar
      with their point of view, ask them to help you fill it out.

      If you do not know and you do not know someone who knows
      them, then ask yourself this question: "If I had their job and was
      making their promises, how would I fill this out?"
3. After filling out both forms, ask the following questions:
   a. If they read what you wrote about their point of view, would they
      feel heard and valued?
   b. What did you learn?
   c. What intersections do you see?
   d. How will this change the next conversation?

For those of you who are interested, more on the Presence-Empathy Deep
Dive can be found online at *thevitalityimperative.com/explore*.

Empathy Principle #3: Beware the four empathy killers

Empathy is hard to cultivate and easily lost. In our experience, there are four conditions that always threaten empathy in a leader, and by extension the contributions that empathy affords an organization. Those four empathy killers are hurry, stress, position power, and the compulsion to be right and prove others wrong.

1. Hurry

Time pressure leads to hurry, and the hurried miss a lot. In some auto-racing circuits, drivers are paired with "spotters" who sit high in the stands and watch the track environment around the driver. The driver moving at 150 to 200 miles per hour simply cannot see what the spotter sees. That partnership is crucial to safety and success. When you feel hurried, take a breath and then enroll your own spotter. Whom do you trust to help you spot threats to empathy and insight?

2. Stress

When we're under stress, our survival instincts take over. The amygdala, a brain center essential to our drive to survive, kicks in and within three seconds cortisol and adrenaline flood the brain. At this point, we choose to fight, flee, freeze, or appease. An effective, empathetic leader can recognize these stress indicators, recover presence, and, in turn, the drive to socialize, and have both drives engaged in the face of the challenge. Here is how:

- Notice the stress and take a deep, centering breath.
- Name the "survive" reaction: is it to fight, flee, freeze, or appease?
- Ask, "What am I *for* that seems to be at risk?"
- Ask, "What do I have to give to others, and what do I need to get from others?"
- Ask, "What is important now?"

Noticing and naming the stress, and then recovering what you have to contribute, tends to reinvigorate the socialize drive and evoke empathy for yourself and others.

3. Position Power

The University of California, Berkeley's Greater Good Science Center sponsors research into the human roots of compassion and altruism. The center reports that, "Research has shown that attaining higher socioeconomic status diminishes empathy, perhaps because people of high socioeconomic status have less of a need to connect with, rely on, and cooperate with others."

We think that an increase in position power has similar impact. As we gain more position power, we tend to forget what it is like to be on the lower rungs of the leadership ladder. The lesson is simple: the greater your authority, the more conscious and deliberate you will need to be about recognizing, respecting, and intersecting with others.

Always remember, people *choose* wholehearted contribution. It cannot be demanded. The greatest contributions humans make are always given, not taken.

4. The Compulsion to be Right and Prove Others Wrong

According to *Psychology Today*, "When a person has a compulsion, he is trapped in a pattern of repetitive and senseless thinking." One of the pervasive human compulsions is irrational, rapid judgement. Within microseconds, we assess behavior, ascribe motivations, and decide if someone is good or bad, right or wrong. Rash judgment cuts off a chance to understand yourself, others, and the circumstances we share.

A wild suggestion: the next time you catch yourself quickly disapproving of another, take a breath, recover presence and empathy, and learn something worthy of your regard.

Your
Vitality Imperative

Earlier, we asked you to keep a real challenge in mind as you move through the book. Regarding your *vitality imperative:*

- Are there any people you disapprove of or criticize?

- Are there any people who are resisting your priorities and ideas?

- Who shows up on both lists? Those people are perfect opportunities for improving empathy.

Practicing Empathy: What you can do to improve

Each of these practices is tried and true for improving empathy. But before you pick a practice to try, recall your *vitality imperative.*

Empathy Practice #1: An appreciation audit

Appreciation improves empathy. Once per week, for six to eight weeks, think about three or four people you appreciate.

For each person, ask:

- What do I admire?

- For what am I grateful?

- Do they know how they have contributed to me?

- If not, what will I do, and by when, to make sure they know?

We have found that simply being present to people we appreciate makes empathy more easily available.

Empathy Practice #2: A curiosity challenge

Think of someone with whom you interact frequently, such as a personal or professional acquaintance. What is something they are very interested in that you are not? Set aside thirty minutes and get curious about the subject. Then:

- *Listen to learn:* find something interesting about the area. What is something you would be willing to know more about?

- *Give them an opportunity to contribute:* tell the other person about your area of interest and ask them to teach you something.

Empathy Practice #3: A resistance audit

From your *vitality imperative*, note who showed up on both lists—your list of people of whom you disapprove and your list of people resisting you. Then do the following:

- Regarding your *vitality imperative*, fill out a Presence-Empathy Deep Dive for yourself.

- Then ask yourself:
  - How have I disappointed them?
  - How might they criticize me?
  - What priorities or ideas of theirs do I resist?

- For each person, consider the following: What did you learn? When will you talk to them next? What will change about how you interact?

Vitality Is Increased When Empathy Is Practiced

In many professional settings, practicing empathy is unusual. Those leaders who make the practice habitual, however, tend to become more curious and less opinionated. And, as those they lead feel more understood and valued, they become more candid and trusting. As a result, organizational and personal impasses transform into intersections. The result is a substantial decrease in stress and a measurable increase in contributions per employee.

So, what do you say? Are you willing to practice empathy?

Here are some questions worth considering as you decide whether or not you want to promise empathy in your personal and professional life:

- Where is it important for me to be empathetic?
- How does the quality of my empathy help or hurt the connections that build *community*?
- How does my empathy help or hurt people making a significant *contribution*?
- How does my empathy help or hurt people making a *choice* to do great work?
- How can I develop more empathy today? What, if anything, will I do differently?

For more on empathy, go to ***thevitalityimperative.com/empathy***. You will find resources and practices, including those already referenced here, to advance your empathic abilities.

PROMISE #3

PURPOSE:

The Mutual Resolve of a Community

Yet the ancients knew something which we seem to have forgotten.
All means prove but a blunt instrument, if they have not behind them
a living spirit.

—Albert Einstein

The secret of success is constancy to purpose.

—Benjamin Disraeli

Back in the mid-1980s, there was an economic collapse in the United States. Texas, in particular, was a financial mess. The price of oil had collapsed, and the cascading effects were brutal. Altogether, Texas banks lost close to $1 billion per quarter, and bankruptcies were filed at a record pace.

During that time, one of us had a major stake in a business that was in arrears on state sales tax. The case officer said if we didn't pay the back taxes within thirty days, they would close our business and auction off our equipment. The business owners offered to put up real estate holdings as collateral to secure repayment of the taxes, but that was rejected as a solution. Talking with the case officer's supervisor yielded a similar, inflexible threat.

As the deadline approached, one of the business owners went to the Texas State Capitol and asked to see the comptroller. With no appointment, it was highly unlikely he'd get a face-to-face meeting. But desperation was motivation, and the owner sat for hours until someone agreed to see him.

A woman appeared, said she was an assistant comptroller and a direct report to the comptroller, and offered to meet. The owner repeated all he had said previously to the case officers. Five hundred jobs were at stake in a time when Texas jobs were precious. Operating costs had been cut, and there was a plausible plan to repay the taxes. The state would lose out on future tax revenues with the business gone. And there was real estate to pledge that showed good faith. After forty-five minutes of examining the current business performance and plan for repayment, the official agreed to forestall the asset seizure and allow the business to continue.

As he was leaving her offices the owner said, "You are a godsend, and I am very grateful. I have a question, though: why, after hours of discussions, were we refused by the case officer and the supervisor, and yet you and I could reach an agreement in only forty-five minutes?"

"I've been thinking about that during the time you and I have been talking," she said. "I'll need to convene some others to decide what the implications are because I've realized something: when the field personnel are faced with a problem, they simply look at the manual and follow the instructions. When I'm faced with a problem, I look at what is best for the state of Texas. I think we can do a better job of teaching others to do the same thing."

The assistant comptroller had a distinct and genuine purpose to support the economic welfare of the state of Texas. This purpose made her thinking clear, and as she and the business owner shifted from adversaries to allies, a path forward emerged with unexpected speed. That is the power of purpose.

This highlights some crucial truths: process without purpose causes frustrating, wasteful bureaucracy. Metrics that lack purpose become irrelevant to the people doing the work. And wasteful bureaucracy plus unimportant work is a recipe for low engagement, low productivity, and high supervision costs.

How Does Purpose Produce More with Less?

If you prefer an inspired, resilient workforce instead of meaningless mechanics and micromanagement, then it's time you harnessed the power of purpose for your organization.

The tangible benefits of purpose to community, contribution, and choice are many:

- *Purpose makes work meaningful* and, in turn, deepens accountability.
- *Purpose promotes teamwork* by clarifying a common, worthy future.
- *Purpose improves performance management* and lowers supervision costs.
- *Purpose improves and accelerates decision making* by clarifying decision criteria.
- *Purpose improves personal devotion* and, in turn, resilience and agility.
- *Purpose promotes constructive debate* because people argue for the purpose rather than against each other.

Purpose Principle #1: Separate purpose from methods and measurable goals

In a 1961 address before Congress, U.S. President John F. Kennedy famously said, "I believe that this nation should commit itself to achieving the goal, before this decade is out, of landing a man on the moon and returning him safely to earth."

Many have lauded that statement as the source of the space program achievements that followed, using it as evidence that it is best to, as Stephen Covey says, begin with the end in mind. However, Kennedy's statement is *not* the source of those amazing accomplishments. Here's why.

Earlier in his address, Kennedy said:

Finally, if we are to win the battle that is now going on around the world between freedom and tyranny, the dramatic achievements in space which occurred in recent weeks should have made clear to us all, as did the Sputnik in 1957, the impact of this adventure on the minds of men everywhere, who are attempting to make a determination of which road they should take. . . . Recognizing the head start obtained by the Soviets with their large rocket engines, which gives them many months of lead-time, and recognizing the likelihood that they will exploit this lead for some time to come in still more impressive successes, we nevertheless are required to make new efforts on our own. For while we cannot guarantee that we shall one day be first, we can guarantee that any failure to make this effort will make us last. . . . But this is not merely a race.

Space is open to us now; and our eagerness to share its meaning is not governed by the efforts of others. We go into space because whatever mankind must undertake, free men must fully share.

In the 1960s, Congress wasn't just throwing money willy-nilly at any program, let alone some crazy mission to go to the moon. There were far better things to spend taxpayer money on. No, the purpose was not just a mere adventure in space but to secure our freedom. Freedom was something Congress knew was worth the cost. Kennedy stood for space exploration as an imminent field of action for the victory of freedom over tyranny. It was that urgent purpose that led to our investment and communal commitment to the goal of "landing a man on the moon and returning him safely to earth." The creative tension caused by an urgent, relevant purpose and a clear, aspirational goal led to unprecedented, successful methods.

Put simply, goals clarify measurable achievement, methods clarify how we will get there, and purpose is the reason those goals and methods matter and the source of our drive to achieve. It was not merely the goal of landing on the moon that led to success. Rather, it was the interplay of purpose, method, and goals that fueled the triumph for Kennedy and the U.S. space program.

Work without purpose is lifeless—and costly. Goals without purpose raise supervision costs and stifle commitment and intelligence. Methods and processes without purpose are the fast track to bureaucratic waste. But when purpose is married to work, it enlivens people and elevates performance.

Purpose Principle #2: **Purpose is what you are for, and worries are what you are against**

As we touched on in our chapter on empathy, purposes are expressed in terms of what you are for rather than what you are against.

Bob Johansen has led the Institute for the Future, a preeminent forecasting consultancy, through forty years of remarkably accurate predictions. In fact, the institute is the only organization of its kind to outlive its first ten years of forecasts. In his prescient book *Leaders Make the Future*, Johansen says that it is important to harness our inner drive "to build and grow things, as well as connect with others in the making. Leaders need this basic skill to make and remake organizations."

Johansen refers to this skill as the "maker instinct." In our work all over the world, we have found that the maker instinct is unleashed when people are focused on what they are for.

We know a ski and snowboard instructor who helps illustrate this point. He says injuries, both slight and serious, happen when people focus on what they are against.

"Imagine you are at the top of a wooded hill and the way down requires skiing through the trees," he says. "The worst guidance you can give is 'Whatever you do, don't hit a tree!' As soon as someone hears that, their attention is on what they are against, not what they are for. Soon, people are running into trees."

Rather than focusing on the trees, this instructor asks skiers to focus on where they want to go. "I ask people to look for sunlit, open space and visually make a path for themselves," he continues. "When they are focused on well-lit, open space, they easily move through the trees. It is safer and more efficient to focus on what we do want than what we don't."

Spend some time turning your worries into purposes and notice the difference. Some examples:

- "I'm against silos and turf protection," to "I'm for cross-boundary collaboration."
- "I'm against time-wasting bureaucracy," to "I'm for processes that make the right thing easy and the wrong thing hard."
- "I'm against embarrassing leaks to the press," to "I'm for being the source of information rather than the subject of gossip."
- "I'm against competitors copying our products and services," to "I'm for always-on innovation."

Turning a worry into a purpose is an essential part of achieving more with less time, money, and stress, and it's directly related to improving performance. This isn't just feel-good, folksy wisdom. Rather, it's what the leading minds in business research are confirming. As Carolyn B. Aiden and

Scott P. Keller write in their *McKinsey Quarterly* article "The CEO's Role in Leading Transformation:"

> *University of Wisconsin researchers who were conducting a study of the adult-learning process videotaped two bowling teams during several games. The members of each team then studied their efforts on video to improve their skills. But the two videos had been edited differently. One team received a video showing only its mistakes; the other team's video, by contrast, showed only the good performances. After studying the videos, both teams improved their game, but the team that studied its successes improved its score twice as much as the one that studied its mistakes. Evidently, focusing on the errors can generate feelings of fatigue, blame, and resistance. Emphasizing what works well and discussing how to get more out of those strengths taps into creativity, passion, and the desire to succeed.*

Purpose Principle #3: **Align people to purpose**

In any organization, there are many competing purposes that can either help or hurt the overall organizational purpose. Aligning people to your organization's ultimate purpose requires researching the various priorities in your organization and showing how they intersect with the organization's purposes. Many great performance stories feature this core accomplishment.

In 2006, Bill Ford convinced Alan Mulally to leave Boeing and succeed him as CEO of the Ford Motor Company. At the time, the U.S. auto industry and Ford itself were in financial disarray. Given the stress of the times, the various stakeholders in the company were narrowly focused on their own interests. Mulally faced a challenging question: how could he bring customers, investors, suppliers, Ford executives, employees, union partners, and government leaders together to turn around the company?

Mulally spent the first few months researching Ford's situation, including the priorities and pain points of the stakeholders. Among the many concerns were cutting costs, raising capital, restoring respect to the brand, avoiding government intervention, keeping experienced talent, increasing pay and benefits, growing the stock price, protecting personal careers, fostering product pride, and generating more autonomy in decision making.

Mulally spoke with people when and where he could: in cafeterias, hallways, informal conversations, and formal meetings. After all that research, he concluded it was time for Ford to "merge with ourselves." He was ready to propose a direction that best served the interests of all the stakeholders. He ultimately called the purpose One Ford, and it featured three priorities:

1. *People:* A skilled and motivated workforce
2. *Products:* Detailed customer knowledge and focus
3. *Productivity:* A lean global enterprise

Mulally was a tireless proponent of the One Ford vision. He believed wholeheartedly that it was responsive to all stakeholder needs. He invited people to get behind the new direction and said, "Everyone loves a comeback story. Let's work together to write the best one ever." Mulally was devoted to aligning people around a purpose that served the entire Ford community.

You can read about Mulally's revitalization of Ford in greater detail in Bryce G. Hoffman's brilliant book about the turnaround, *An American Icon: Alan Mulally and the Fight to Save Ford Motor Company.* Hoffman writes, "Instead of figuring out whom to get rid of, he was trying to figure out where each of Ford's executives could make the biggest contribution to the company's turnaround effort."

And it worked. Under Mulally's leadership, Ford became the most profitable car company in the world and was the only major American auto manufacturer to steer clear of the bailout provided by the U.S. government to Ford's competitors in 2008 and 2009.

And it all started with a commitment to align people to purpose.

Purpose Principle #4: **Make purpose the boss**

A Vitality leader always strives to make the right thing easy and the wrong thing hard. Key to success in this effort is making purpose the boss rather than any one person.

When a person is the boss—the Superior Leader model—conflicts escalate to that powerful person. When you make purpose the boss—the Connected Leader model—people refer to the purpose to resolve differences. As a result, they make their own decisions and get work done quickly and independently.

The December 2011 issue of *Harvard Business Review (HBR)* featured a fascinating article by Gary Hamel titled, "First, Let's Fire All the Managers." In the article, Hamel featured Morning Star, a very profitable, rapidly growing food processor, as a prime example of a company that makes "the mission the boss," creating a culture where team members "will be self-managing professionals, initiating communications and the coordination of their activities with fellow colleagues, customers, suppliers, and fellow industry participants, absent directives from others."

In the article, Morning Star President Chris Rufer highlights the economic benefit of their high-purpose, low-bureaucracy approach. As Hamel writes, "Over the past twenty years, Morning Star's volumes, revenues, and profits have grown at a double-digit clip, claims Rufer. Industry growth, by contrast, has averaged 1 percent a year."

More on low-bureaucracy, high-purpose organizations is available online at *thevitalityimperative.com/explore*.

The more a work environment is designed to serve purpose rather than hierarchy, the easier it is to get work done. Our research into purpose-driven companies leads us to prescribe three areas of focus: (1) signature actions, (2) signature decisions, and (3) helping work get done.

Signature Actions

The actions of people with position power and influence are signs in any organization. To make purpose the boss, take visible, signature actions that prove your devotion as a leader to purpose. The following are a few suggestions for signature actions.

Share Stories about True-to-Purpose Challenges

Illuminate moments that test commitment to purpose. For example, the Customer Value Store started in 1963 as a health and beauty product discounter. Over the next fifty years, CVS Health evolved into a health care giant. CEO Larry Merlo led the company through a challenging choice in 2014: should it give up $2 billion in annual cigarette sales to be true to their purpose of reinventing pharmacy to have a more active, supportive role in health care? The answer was yes. Every time Merlo and others tell this story, colleagues, customers, investors, and the press take new, respectful notice of CVS.

Practice Purpose-Led Performance Management

Who around you produces results by being true to purpose? Acknowledge them, reward them, and make sure the word gets out. Conversely, who is clearly violating your purpose? What actions, as a signature of your leadership, will you take to address those violations?

Hire and Promote for Purpose

The next time you hire or promote someone in your organization, do research on purpose, not just skills. Some questions to ask are:

- Will you please tell me about one of your most satisfying work experiences? For you, what was important about that experience?

- Why are you interested in this job? What makes it personally important to you?

- Will you tell me about one of your most disappointing work experiences? What did you learn? For you, what is important about those lessons?

- For you, what is important about your career? Why does that matter to you?

Look for the themes that run through the answers. Those themes are windows into the purposes of the person you are interviewing.

- Tell them the themes you see and ask if those are accurate.
- Share the purposes that matter most to you.
- Share the purposes that matter most to your organization.

Look together for a natural intersection between their purpose, yours, and the enterprise's.

When candidate skills are comparable, make alignment with purpose the tiebreaker. Hire for purpose and make it public.

Signature Decisions

When you use a clear purpose to establish decision criteria, something remarkable happens: people argue for the criteria, not against one another. This frees people up to say what they really think and leads to honest, healthy debate and better decisions. Do this with decisions that many people care about and your purpose will take root quickly and deeply.

Back in the mid-1990s, a major international company had a problem: how to get more of a very popular product line into the hands of European customers. The products were shipped from Asia, North America, and Latin America, which added a lot of cost to the European end user. It became clear there was a need for a production plant that would reduce these shipping costs. Additionally, there was a need for speed because European competitors were looming. Deciding where to put the new plant, however, was a source of much internal discussion, and the location process was time consuming.

The executive in charge of international manufacturing hosted conversations with all involved in the site's decision process. As he scanned for the intersection between all the points of view, a purpose emerged: a lower-cost breakthrough in availability that substantially improved customer satisfaction, customer use, and productivity.

The people giving input on the decision worked together to turn that purpose into decision criteria. Staying carefully true to the purpose, here are the six criteria for a site they identified:

1. Access to talent
2. Ease of access and cost of transportation
3. Beneficial tax environment
4. Enthusiastic local and national government support
5. Proximity to model customer communities
6. Low labor costs

The team then looked again at the sites in question, rating each of them relative to each of the six criteria as an advantage, neutral, or disadvantage. Then each person explained his or her ratings to the group. Instead of the previous discussions surrounding personal preferences, a spirited debate based on the criteria took place. Thanks to their devotion to the purpose rather than preference, the decision was made quickly, and everyone involved was able to explain and understand the choice.

Helping Work Get Done

The most telling evidence of organizational culture is how work gets done. If the way people are working is off-purpose, then get intimately acquainted with the work and what it takes to do it.

Around 2010, Telstra, the iconic Australian telecommunications and media company, went through a major change. Then-CEO David Thodey was a passionate proponent of the shift from telecommunications monopoly to a nimble, competitive, customer-centric enterprise. The previous CEO uttered similar words to no avail because customer-service ratings were so low that some Telstra employees were embarrassed to tell people where they worked. A major source of complaints came from the customer call centers.

Thodey and his executive team did something that got the attention of the entire company: they went to work in a call center. With a videographer on hand, Thodey and team were trained to take calls, resolve customer complaints, and generally do the work of a call-center employee. The experience was illuminating.

One executive said, "We had no idea how hard it was to give a customer a great experience. We confronted processes, metrics, and policies that made the wrong thing easy and the right thing hard. We were all really affected, and we went to work to get our policies, procedures, and measures more aligned with our service purpose."

While things didn't change overnight, employees all over Telstra heard about the executives' project and many saw the videos. Transformation plans were improved and the service purpose got more traction. Today, Telstra is a respected example for shifting a culture. Thodey and the executive team did the work to align the system with the real demands of work. They made the purpose the boss.

Purpose Principle #5: **Keep purpose alive**

A car wheel out of alignment wears out more quickly, causes greater fuel consumption, and makes for a rough ride. All these things are improved by simply aligning the wheel. It's the same with purpose in an organization: when purpose is alive, intention and attention are aligned. That alignment makes more good things happen with less time, money, and stress. We call this leadership imperative to keep attention and intention aligned *purposeful presence*.

Purposeful presence is a function of an always-on question: where is our purpose now?

Our purpose attracts attention in three ways:

1. *Rationally:* Do we have a clear strategic story that is omnipresent, easy to understand, and easy to tell?

2. *Emotionally:* Are we appreciating and acknowledging contributions? Are we respecting the choices people make to commit personally to our enterprise's purpose? Are we staying in touch with what is important about our work?

3. *Physically:* Are we continually evolving our circumstances to make the right thing easy and the wrong thing hard? As a leader, is my body aligned with the words I say?

Attitude and action are correlated to what is present. If you notice off-purpose attitudes and actions, you can bet that purpose is losing presence—and, like a flame without fuel, it is quickly dying. In order to breathe new life, ask, "Where is my purpose now?"

Practicing Purpose:
What you can do to improve

Leading from purpose is a promise worth keeping. Every leader has work to do in being purposeful and maintaining organizational purpose. We have yet to meet anyone who is perfect! Consider these three ways to consciously practice championing purpose in your life and organization.

Purpose Practice #1:
A purpose-method-goal audit

Answer these questions about your *vitality imperative*:

1. Do have a purpose for your challenge?

    a. If yes, what is the purpose?

    On a scale of 1 to 10, how important is the purpose to you? What explains your rating?

    On a scale of 1 to 10, how important is the purpose to other people essential to success? What explains your rating?

    b. If no, move to #2.

2. Do you have a measurable goal or goals? If so, what are they?

    a. For you, what is important about the goal(s)? (Ask and answer at least three times.)

    b. For others, what is important about the goal(s)? (Ask and answer
      at least three times.)

    c. How will you measure success? What early warning measures will
      keep you alert along the way?

3. Does your method of success connect purpose and goal?

    a. Are your methods true to purpose? If not, what actions will you
      take?

    b. Are you confident in your plan? If not, what actions will you take?

This quick audit is an occasion for reflection. As you answer the questions, consider the following:

- A plan driven by mutual purpose requires less supervision than "ordinary" plans.

- A mutual purpose accelerates the development of goals and methods

If purpose seems unclear, uninspired, or unshared in your answers, you can handle that in the next purpose practice.

Purpose Practice #2: Discovering collective purpose

The vast majority of people want their work to matter, and that deep desire is a reliable path to discovery.

Years ago, Richard Rianoshek, cofounder of Conversant and the co-author of our last book, *The Communication Catalyst*, came up with a simple method for identifying collective purpose. We call this tool a Conversation Prep Chart, and the people of Conversant have helped thousands of our clients use the chart to discover mutual purpose.

Go to ***thevitalityimperative.com/explore*** for a downloadable version of this tool.

Conversation Prep Chart

Key people	Purposes (for)	Worries (against)	Circumstances (facts)
Me			
Intersecting themes			
Authentic shared purpose			

Here is how to use the chart:

1. Write a brief situation statement. What is already known about the challenge? Is there any information regarding an already-known purpose, methods, and/or measurable goals?

2. Who, including you, are the five people most essential to your challenge? Look for a few important influencers who understand the interests of many people.

3. For each person, starting with you, write down known purposes (for), concerns (against), and circumstances (facts). You may remember those terms from the empathy work.

    a. For the others, if you know what they would say, use their words to fill out the chart.

    b. If you don't know, who does?

    c. If you don't know someone who knows, imagine you had that person's job. If you did, what would you say?

    d. If all you can see is what someone is against, then ask these questions:

    For him or her, what is important?

    What can he or she be *for* that, if successful, would take care of their concerns?

4. Look down each column and put themes you see in the intersection row. If you see words in common, use those words.

5. Using the words in the three intersection boxes, write a purpose statement that would be important to all five of you.

6. Imagine writing an email to each person inviting them to a meeting featuring the purpose you composed. Would they want to attend? If so, you are on the right track. If not, you have probably missed something important to the person or persons who would not attend. Who could help you redo the chart?

Resources describing how to use the same principles to discover purpose for large groups, even entire large organizations, are available online at **thevitalityimperative.com/explore**.

Purpose Practice #3: Recovering purpose with glad-sad-mad

Sometimes people live through periods of disappointment that destroy their connection to purpose. Is anyone related to your *vitality imperative* alienated or otherwise disconnected from the work at hand? If so, you may want to host a glad-sad-mad debrief:

1. Prepare three flip charts: one entitled "Glad," another "Sad," and another "Mad."

2. Have three different-colored 3" x 5" Post-it notepads, one for each chart.

3. Define terms and give instructions:

   a. *Glad:* Something you are happy about that is related to the topic of the debrief. Please write one to three "glad" notes on separate Post-its and place on the Glad chart.

   b. *Sad:* Something you are unhappy about that, while you don't like it, you are ready to put it behind you. Please write one to three "sad" notes and place on Sad chart.

   c. *Mad:* Something you are unhappy about that is, for you, an occasion for action. Write one to three notes and place on the Mad chart.

4. If the group is small enough (fifteen or fewer) have each person say what they put on the charts, why it is important to them, any lessons they think are worth learning, any actions they plan to take, and any requests they have of others.

5. If the group is large, have people tour the charts. Then, in table groups, have each person follow the instructions in Step 4 above.

6. Have each person write down their answer to this question: "Given all we just said, heard, and learned, what remains important to you about our challenge?"

7. Post the answers, look for intersections, and renew a common purpose.

Resources describing how to host the glad-sad-mad experience for very large groups are available online at ***thevitalityimperative.com/explore***.

Here are some questions worth considering as you decide whether or not you want to promise purpose in your personal and professional life:

- What is the true purpose for my *vitality imperative*? Where am I focusing on methods and goals without purpose? How will I adjust?

- What are we collectively for? Is purpose the boss? How much of our energies are focused on what we are against instead of what we are for?

- How does purpose strengthen *community*?

- How does purpose unleash *contribution*?

- How does purpose inspire *choice*?

- Have I learned anything from this chapter that is relevant and useful? What, if anything, will I do differently?

For further resources on purpose, including the resources and practices listed here, visit ***thevitalityimperative.com/purpose***.

Next, we turn to authenticity, where we will discover that the truth is an appetite many have yet to acquire. Vitality leaders, on the other hand, are hungry for it.

PROMISE #4

AUTHENTICITY:

Accelerating Achievement through Truth

*In a room where people unanimously maintain a conspiracy of silence,
a single word of truth sounds like a pistol shot.*

—Czeslaw Milosz

*The origin of all conflict between me and my fellow-men is that
I do not say what I mean, and that I do not do what I say. For this
confuses and poisons, again and again and in increasing measure,
the situation between myself and the other.*

—Martin Buber, *The Way of Man*

*Our most important job as leaders was to communicate openly
and transparently with our global teams, taking each and every one
of our…associates on the journey with us.*

—Angela Ahrendts, SVP Retail and Online Stores, Apple

In 2012, The New York Times published a gripping and disturbing multimedia
article by John Branch titled, "Snow Fall: The Avalanche at Tunnel Creek."
Branch's piece won the 2013 Pulitzer Prize for feature writing. It's a prime
example of truth as a casualty of avoidance and the dire consequences.

The article tells the story of sixteen backwoods experts, including pro skiers
and skiing insiders from media, manufacturing, and apparel organizations
who had gathered to ski a legendary, out-of-bounds powder run called
Tunnel Creek in the Cascade Range east of Seattle, Washington. One

said later, "This was a crew that seemed like it was assembled by some higher force."

If you read "Snow Fall," you will see that some had reservations about the run. The recent, heavy snow was as potentially dangerous as it was beautiful. Yet, some did not speak up because those more famous and skilled did not seem worried.

Members of the party did not want to seem "whiny" and decided not to make a fuss, thinking, "There's no way this entire group can make a decision that isn't smart. . . It's got to be fine." The social pressure and potential embarrassment suppressed the worries, and in the end three people died, one was injured, and the trauma to family and friends was, and is, immeasurable.

How Does Authenticity Produce More with Less?

We've asked thousands of people around the world if they prefer the truth, however painful, over avoidance and deception. The overwhelming majority say yes.

However, the biology of fear interferes with this longing for honesty. This lack of authenticity results in appalling and systemic problems caused by self-deception, avoidance, "spin," and outright lying.

In an organization that keeps the promise of authenticity, there is a free expression of truth, even against the groupthink. And it is this expression of truth that creates avenues for true achievement and success.

Candor, however, does have the power to both help and harm. Helpful authenticity is not just blurting out what is on your mind. Rather, it has two crucial, skillful components: (1) discovering and (2) telling the truth with the intent to be constructive not destructive.

No matter how pristine your integrity, those two areas of skill are important to develop. Keeping the authenticity promise is as much about competence as it is about character, because our good intentions are not enough.

The tangible benefits of authenticity are many:

- *Authenticity creates trust.* As Covey says, "Business moves at the speed of trust."

- *Authenticity elevates the intelligence of a group.* Any group is potentially smarter than the individuals in that group if we speak openly and listen curiously to difference.

- *Authenticity accelerates solution.* If knowledge is shared, everything moves faster, including problem solving.

- *Authenticity improves agility and resilience,* which demand fact-based and purpose-driven honesty. Rate of adjustment is a great competitive advantage if the adjustments are based on reality.

- *Authenticity inspires innovation.* People honestly connected to reality and one another become creative allies.

- *Authenticity reduces stress.* When we know that information is honest and colleagues are candid, worry declines. We are less suspicious about misinformation and hidden agendas. Our attention is more on achievement and less on hidden, worrisome threats.

Leaders who promise and deliver authenticity achieve more with less time, money, and stress. Let's get into why.

Authenticity Principle #1: Truth accelerates success and fear decelerates truth

A business executive we know received a letter from an attorney accusing him of violating a nondisclosure agreement (NDA). The NDA covered the intellectual property of a company he had considered but decided against buying. Our friend knew the accusation was untrue and had a conversation with the attorney to resolve the misunderstanding. It did not go well.

The meeting featured interruptions, accusations, and arguments. The tone was suspicious and sarcastic. The executive decided that the time was fruitless and declined to talk further without his own attorney present. Three weeks and two more meetings later the only results were legal bills with no resolution in sight.

In a finger-pointing tirade, the accusing attorney cited a previous legal case to support his position. Our friend recognized the name of one of the attorneys involved in the previous case. "I'm familiar with that law firm," he said. "Do you know Will Miller? I think he handled it personally."

"Of course I know Will!" came the angry reply. "We know each other well. In fact, he has been a mentor of mine."

"OK, then I have a prerequisite for any further discussions with you. Call Will, tell him about our conflict, and get his input. Otherwise, I'll see you in court."

The attorney left the room to make the call. He returned in less than ten minutes, and the mood was different. "Let's start again, summarize each of our positions, and see if we can find a path forward," suggested the attorney.

They did exactly that. In just over an hour they agreed to information sharing between the two companies, and they also agreed that there had been no NDA violation. The nearly month-long impasse was resolved with that one phone call.

As they were leaving the conference room, the executive asked, "What did Will say when you called?"

"He said he knew you well and that, if it were him, he would put aside suspicion and replace it with factual inquiry. He said to protect my client's interests without assuming you are a liar."

When the attorney put aside his fear of being deceived and conned, it was like a dam broke, allowing authenticity to flow through. This commitment to authenticity paved the way for quick resolution.

Most of us have felt deceived, conned, and manipulated. Those disappointments set us up to be careful with what we disclose and cautious about what we believe. However, each of us also enjoys relationships that are open, trusting, and free. How can we have less of the former and more of the latter? It starts with understanding the source of deception.

For the vast majority of us, pretense, or, withholding relevant information or outright lying, is a response to a threat or a potential one. This leads us to a simple truth: if you want to reduce the dishonesty around you, reduce threats—real or perceived.

Reducing dishonesty requires the presence to notice threat and fear, empathy for those who are grappling with stress from real or perceived threats, and smart action to disarm those threats and free the truth.

Here is a course of action to get the conversation to move out of pretense:

1. *Take the helm:* "I'm steering this conversation. How will I change my conduct in order to change theirs?"

2. *Respect the threat:* "What is dangerous for them or for me? Is it position power? Possible exposure or embarrassment? Fear of being conned? Fear of being excluded? What else?"

3. *Pierce the pretense:* With calm respect, say the potential dangers out loud. Here are some examples.

    a. "If I were you, I'd be suspicious of me if only because of my title."

    b. "This could look like a setup for blame. Please help me make it about working together to make things better."

    c. "We have been terrible at including and learning from people who know the work best, like you."

4. *Ask and learn:* With genuine, relaxed curiosity, ask a question they would like to answer, such as, "Is there anything in our company that is making your work difficult?" or "What do you wish others understood about your situation?" Say what you learned, ask another question, and repeat.

The first three steps are to name and diminish the threat. The last step gets people talking and, as you learn, they will begin to disclose new information. As a word of warning, if people have felt suppressed for a while, the things they say may come out in a wave of pent-up emotion. Although it may not feel like that in the moment, the emotional torrent is far preferable to pretense. How to react is covered in the next principle.

Authenticity Principle #2: The speed of opinion is faster than the speed of understanding

Over the last thirty years, our research has unearthed three kinds of honesty: (1) sincere opinion, (2) accurate, fact-based inquiry, and (3) authentic values, purposes, and priorities. Principle #2 addresses the first: sincere opinion.

How quickly do we form opinions? Around the world, the most frequent response is, "Instantly."

How quickly do people understand an important point you are trying to make? Does it take longer than the speed of opinion? The answer is invariably, "Yes."

This brings us to a major challenge in making vital connections: people form opinions prior to understanding. The following story illustrates the destructive power of irrational, rapid opinion.

In the early 1980s, Narayan Murthy led a division of Patni Computer Systems (PCS) in India. One of the Patni brothers who did not normally interact with Murthy gave him an order. Murthy, realizing the brother did not understand the activities in his division, resisted the instruction and wanted to discuss the reasons. Mr. Patni refused, saying, "Just do what you are told to do."

In the wake of this disinterested refusal, Murthy decided to leave PCS. Nandan Nilekani and others followed him out, and they formed Infosys. In 2014, Infosys enjoyed $8 billion in revenue. The Patni brothers ultimately descended into sibling rivalry, and PCS was sold to U.S.-based iGate Corporation. An authority figure with an ill-informed opinion drove off great talent who spawned a company more successful than his own.

When sincere opinion trumps available data, it nearly always leads to terrible results. Many people think positively of the word "sincere" and may question our use of the word here, but we use it intentionally. Sincerity, while noble, can often be disconnected from reality. It's quite possible for someone to be sincerely wrong. Just ask yourself, "Has anyone believed something about me that isn't true?" We can all answer yes. Those people were sincere, but they were also wrong. As Dr. Martin Luther King Jr. said, "Nothing in all the world is more dangerous than sincere ignorance and conscientious stupidity."

Chernobyl and Fukushima nuclear disasters, and the Challenger and Columbia space shuttle explosions, all included fact-based worries that were minimized or ignored. The meltdowns at Enron, Tyco, and other companies are case studies in how arrogant, sincere opinions can destroy value. HP's poor acquisition decisions regarding Palm, Electronic Data Systems, and Autonomy all included internal disputes that were not resolved by fact-based discussion but instead by the opinions of people in powerful positions.

As you think through your *vitality imperative*, ask, "Do I or others have sincere opinions that are short circuiting our potential for success?" If so, write them down, and make a plan to address them.

There are ways to upgrade sincere opinion to a fact-based inquiry. One good prerequisite is the emotional practice we call "Name It," an exercise we covered in the chapter on presence. As you become reliable for naming and shifting your emotions, your emotional agility will be a big help in converting sincere opinion into valuable conversation.

Your **Vitality Imperative:**
Who has sincere, immovable opinions?

Take a moment and note anyone who has a strongly held opinion related to your *vitality imperative*. Then note any of those opinions in conflict with your own, e.g. "This new process will make our sales force more effective," versus, "This process will make sales people data-driven predators and push our customers to the competition."

Pick one sincerely opinionated conflict, and schedule a time to get together with the opinionated parties. Then, follow these steps:

1. *Pick a venue.* The greater the disagreement, the more human senses need to be engaged in order to dislodge opinion. For instance, email and texts engage only our eyesight before generating perceptions and reactions. Email and texts, then, are terrible for resolving disagreements. Voice adds an audible element that allows people to perceive and react to mood. Web solutions that feature real-time video connections add more senses, and in-person meetings and dinners even more.

2. *Prioritize learning, not agreement.* The priority is for each person to learn what led to the other's strong opinion. This is not about convincing each other to change their minds.

3. *Interview, learn, and verify.* Set the mood through curious, respectful understanding. Listen the way you want them to listen to you. What led to this point of view? Ask the reporter's questions: "What happened? When? Who? Where? Why?" What are you discovering that you did not know before? Summarize what you heard and highlight what you learned.

4. *Switch roles (interviewer to interviewee):* Go through steps 1 – 3 again.

Humans are innate storytellers. If you give people a chance to tell how they came to their opinion, and if you truly learn from them, they will be more interested in your story. The reciprocal interest loosens the grip of opinion, and the parties usually migrate to better-informed positions. The results are strengthened relationships and improved trust.

Sincerity is far preferable to pretense. An openly stated opinion can usually be researched and learned from, and emotions can be challenging when strong opinions are voiced. Avoid being ensnared in the other's *mad*, *sad*, *afraid*, or *ashamed* emotions, and see if you can be *content* with listening and *glad* to learn.

Authenticity Principle #3: Accurate inquiry arouses creativity, storytelling, and action

In this principle, we upgrade honesty from sincere opinion to accurate, fact-based inquiry. Accurate inquiry is the interplay of these four components:

1. *Purpose:* a meaningful intention that assists in separating stories that help from ones that hurt.

2. *Facts:* mutual experiences or observations that can be proven true.

3. *Explanations:* stories that make sense of the facts.

4. *Listening to learn:* researching any situation for potential value.

Let's debrief something that really happened and see how the four components of accurate inquiry play out.

During a project to develop a rubber material that would not deteriorate from exposure to jet aircraft fuels, 3M's Patsy Sherman accidentally spilled fluorochemical rubber on her colleague's tennis shoe. Immediately, Sherman went to work to remove the spot. However, after many attempts, nothing worked.

After apologies were uttered, they discussed the implications. Maybe the now-permanently marked shoe would just be soiled lab wear. Maybe it should be thrown away. Maybe they needed to be more careful in the future. And just maybe there was something to learn about why nothing could remove the spot.

Sherman and her colleague Samuel Smith gravitated to the last story. Delving into the question turned their efforts upside down. Instead of trying to remove the spill, they began to investigate why it worked so well as a protectant. Sherman and Smith's investigation led to a patent, and the patent led to a product we know today as Scotchgard.

Now, let's look at this through the lens of accurate inquiry:

- *Purpose:* Sherman and Smith were committed to uniquely valuable product development. The immediate goal was a rubber material that would not deteriorate from exposure to jet aircraft fuels. However, when that goal was thwarted, the product development purpose was still alive.

- *Facts:* They knew about the spill, the material of the tennis shoe and the ingredients in the fluorochemical rubber, everything they used to try and remove the spot, and that the spot was still there.

- *Explanations:* Possible explanations included an unfortunate mistake to apologize for, a ruined shoe, a shoe still good for lab wear, the need to be more careful, and that maybe there was something to learn.

- *Listening to learn:* They then asked, "Which explanations might help our purpose of product development?" The rest is history.

This simple story and the resulting discovery led to hundreds of millions of dollars in revenue—and a lot of clean couches. There are similar stories about the discovery of penicillin, Velcro, and Post-it Notes. In every case, fact-based curiosity opened new, extraordinary possibilities.

There are four skills essential to accurate, inspiring inquiry. The better you are at these skills, the easier it gets to turn purpose, facts, explanations, and listening to learn into wildly valuable outcomes. They are:

Skill #1: Separating fact from explanation
All progress slows when explanations masquerade as facts. Get vigilant about the difference and you will reduce the time, money, and stress it takes to solve problems.

- *Facts* must be mutually observable and unarguable. Anything that is arguable should be considered an explanation. Just because you believe something strongly does not make it a fact. For example,

"He is irresponsible and disorganized" is not a fact. If one of those strong opinions comes up, investigate: what has actually happened that led to that opinion? A fact might be "He arrived after the scheduled starting time for the last three project meetings, and twice he said he did not have current information about his team's performance."

- *Explanations* are interpretations, deductions, and opinions about what the facts mean. Facts are like stars in the sky and explanations are what turn those stars into constellations.

Skill #2: Performing bias-ectomy

There is no surgery to remove bias, so this is a mental and emotional accomplishment, not a physical one. If you want to confront just how daunting bias removal is, search Wikipedia for a List of Cognitive Biases. You will see more than one hundred examples of bias that make our perceptions inaccurate and decision making irrational.

So, what can we do about such a daunting problem?

There is a useful though challenging remedy: surround yourself with people who think and act very differently than you, give them a voice, and learn from the differences.

Skill #3: Comparing explanations for contribution to purpose

The test for fact is proof. The test for explanation is value. Given our purpose, how valuable is this explanation?

When facing your *vitality imperative*, if you are stuck with your first explanation, get help from other people. Keep purpose present and generate explanations until you see some that inspire useful action.

Skill #4: Storytelling

Stories bring facts to life. Human beings are meaning-makers and storytellers. As some neuroscientists say, our brains are hardwired for storytelling. We've been using stories to share information a heckuva lot longer than we have PowerPoint. Stories can help us or hurt us—when you tell a story, which is happening? The most powerful stories feature *relevant surprise,* something unexpected that is relevant to purpose, emotion, and/or physical circumstance.

There is much written about storytelling. Joseph Campbell's *The Hero with a Thousand Faces* and *The Power of Myth* profoundly influenced storytellers like George Lucas and Steven Spielberg. More recently, neuroscientists in books like John Medina's *Brain Rules* and Diane Ackerman's marvelous *An Alchemy of Mind* are proving that storytelling shapes the human journey and is worth our never-ending interest.

For now, we suggest that you look at your *vitality imperative* through the lens of storytelling:

- What stories are being told about the past? Which ones hurt our work and which ones help?
- What stories are being told about our present situation? Which help? Which hurt?
- What stories are being told about the future? Which inspire success and which suppress it?

Upgrading sincere opinion to accurate facts and energizing explanations reduces stress, builds community, and provokes creative achievement. We recommend that you get good at it. Some interesting, even entertaining, ways to practice are coming your way.

A variety of resources are available online at ***thevitalityimperative.com/explore*** to help you discover how these four skills apply to your *vitality imperative*.

Authenticity Principle #4: Be true to purpose and true to self

Recently, a soon-to-graduate business student asked to interview one of us as part of a final project. First, we addressed a standard set of questions regarding the launch and leadership of successful businesses. Toward the end of the conversation, however, came a unique question: "What important advice do you have for people graduating from business school?"

After a brief pause, I said, "May I start with a statement and then the advice?"

"Sure!" said the student.

"In our work, we think that the heart of commerce is contribution," I said. "A legitimate, sustainable business makes money by contributing to customers, investors, communities, and employees. So the advice has a starting place: contribution. There is a frequent theme these days at graduation ceremonies. Joseph Campbell's 'Follow your bliss' and various versions of 'Do what you love and you'll never work a day in your life' are now regular, impassioned appeals."

"Yeah," she said. "We hear that a lot."

"How helpful has that been to you?"

"Not very."

"At Conversant, we don't think it is very useful either," I said. "We think that the advice is incomplete and misses the relationship between individual self-expression and commerce."

She took a note, looked up, and leaned forward expectantly.

"So, my important advice is this: keep a question alive and explored for your entire career," I said. "The question is, 'What would I love to give that others would love to get?'"

"Wow, that is a different way to think about it," she said.

"If you can build a business or make a career out of finding where what you love to give intersects with what people would love to get, you'll have something most people want."

"What is that?"

"You'll enjoy making a difference and making money at the same time. If you are running a business, you'll sponsor more enjoyable achievement than most companies, all with less time, money, and stress. Businesses built on networks of contribution make good things happen that people are happy to pay for."

When the conversation ended, the business school student said that our advice was the highlight of the interview. I hope she keeps the question alive.

The key to being true to purpose and to self is finding, again and again, the intersection between what your colleagues would love to give and what your customers, investors, and communities would love to get. When you and your organization are operating from that intersection, oversight declines and achievement accelerates. The impact shows up on the profit and loss statements, balance sheets, and cash flow statements. However, pulling this off requires breaking some bad habits. Is it worth it? Absolutely.

If you study organizational processes, it is hard to find any designed to appreciate, cultivate, and orchestrate contribution. We have learned a few things, and we offer them to you. As in most of our suggestions, handle yourself first, and then take care of others. We recommend that you stay awake to:

- *The purpose of work:* What is the essential contribution for your enterprise, your function, your project, or your specific job?

- *Unique, enjoyable contribution:* What does the enjoyable combination of your talents, education, and experience allow you to give? No false humility allowed! Really explore your unique contribution . . . really!

- *The ethics of contribution:* What can only you provide that the people you lead truly need? If you have a prominent leadership position, take this very seriously. When we work with C-level teams, we ask people to:

  - Explore this question individually and as an executive team.

  - Test your insights with the people you lead. What do they say only you can provide?

  - Do a time test: How much of your time is devoted to things other than what only you can do? What do you need to give away or stop doing to make room for your crucial contributions?

  - Change meeting agendas and schedules to assure your crucial contribution.

  - Review and recalibrate frequently. It is amazing how easily your crucial contribution gets out of focus

- *Put it all together:* What portion of your work passes these three tests?

  - Fits the purpose of my work

  - Fits my unique, enjoyable contribution

  - Fits what only I can give that others need to get

If you experience the portion of your work that fits all three to be less than 75 percent, we recommend that you make a plan to improve the percentage. What, over a reasonable time period, can you change? Who will you ask to join you on the inquiry?

We have been repeatedly surprised how much easier the migration to 75 percent is than people expect. If you raise the question with a work community, often others have the same issue, and job descriptions start to evolve as people begin to trade aspects of their work.

Authenticity Principle #5: Raise issues at Point Easy

In our experience authenticity is an art of correction, not perfection. As mentioned earlier, we are frequently hired to address breakdowns in organizational success. In thirty years of that kind of firefighting, we have found the single biggest source of damage is a failure to raise performance issues in a timely, effective way. If the conversation is timely, the cost of correction is low. If the conversation is effective, it inspires valuable action.

Timely conversation: The 3x Imperative

After years of hard-won lessons, we have adopted the 3x Imperative. It is quite simple: if you worry about the same thing three times, you have to bring it up to someone who can do something about it.

The "who can do something" part matters. If you don't raise the issue to people who have a stake in it, then you're merely gossiping, and gossip is cancer to community.

It is amazing how reluctant people can be to bring up an issue. We recently worked with a prominent international company that is suffering a breakdown in results after a prolonged period of success. We did interviews with several hundred managers, and the worries they voiced were startling in their similarity. Over and over, we heard about long-standing, unresolved conflicts between their high-ranking executives regarding strategic priorities, resource allocation, organizational structure, decision rights, and business performance.

The CEO had developed a reputation for being conflict averse, and the chairman had a reputation for avoiding difficult conversations with the CEO. The culture was infected with avoidance and gossip. People were talking about these problems, just not to the people who could do something about them.

As a result, frustrated people in the system worked in enormous stress as they tried to make up for these pervasive dysfunctions. The CEO has now departed. Others in the high-avoidance group are leaving, too. The new CEO and the remaining talented, committed leaders now have a new chance to trade avoidance for authenticity.

One of us, in an effort to get people to truly enact the 3x Imperative, drew the following for a group of executives:

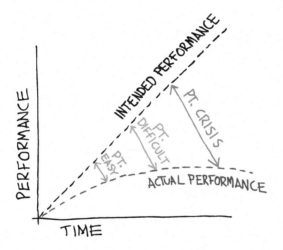

Over time, how likely is it that actual performance deviates from intended performance? Highly likely! The reality is that performance conversations will happen. It is just a question of when.

At Point Easy? If we raise the issue as soon as we are worried about it, there are benefits:

- If people have not lived long in the shortfall, they usually have not descended into blame and shame. So, the conversation tends to be more open.

- The earlier the conversation, the closer we are to the initial deviation. As police detectives have told us, the earlier they are on a case, the better chance they have of solving it.

- People learn that speaking up early is the cultural norm. If I raise an issue early, even if we find there is nothing to be worried about, I'm still reinforcing that, when in doubt, we speak up.

At Point Difficult? Now it gets a bit harder:

- People will have developed impotent explanations, or, ways to explain the situation that are not helping to improve it. As you research these explanations, you will likely trigger defensiveness and blame. Disclosure goes down and time to discovery goes up.

- Once blame sets in, people will often be silo thinkers rather than system thinkers. That makes it harder to work through complex, interrelated challenges and see occasions for valuable action.

- People learn that bringing up issues is difficult, messy, and damaging to relationships.

At Point Crisis? At this point, the problem is public and unavoidable. External forces take over:

- People have developed permanent opinions about who is competent and who is not.

- Credibility of leaders declines because they allowed the issue to linger, fester, and worsen.

- People lose their jobs and a new cast of characters is given a chance to succeed.

The cost of ignoring the 3x Imperative is huge. Organizations reliable for Point Easy conversations will solve the same problems their competitors face, only faster and better.

One impediment to Point Easy reliability is lack of confidence in conversational skill. Let's move to that now.

Effective Conversation and the Conversation Meter

Over twenty years ago, Richard Rianoshek, the co-founder of Conversant, raised an issue.

"People think that there are two choices about communication: speak up or don't. We know that is seriously flawed. People speak up, it doesn't go well, and then they think communication is a bad idea. We have to develop a way for people to catch bad communication in the moment and fix it right away."

And so we did.

Back then we had already done significant work with police departments and military units. Work in those organizations includes SWAT, hostage units, and other special response teams. The women and men who do that kind of work well know something important: the test for communication is action. No excuses. You get the intended action or you don't.

We took all our work to-date and looked at what we'd learned about communicating for action. We were working in a handful of large companies by that time, and we noticed that the same principles applied in police, military, and business settings. We began to explain the principles and techniques by using a deceptively simple model we call the Conversation Meter.

You might notice that all we've covered in this chapter is inherent in the meter:

0– 25	*Pretense:* Lying and withholding. Most pretense is caused by avoiding a threat or a potential one. I fear I can't cope with the consequences of speaking up.
26– 50	*Sincerity:* Honest opinion that comes with the dangerous assumption that my perceptions are accurate. Sincere, opinionated arguments tend to be won by someone with position power, emotional dominance, or physical dominance.
51– 75	*Accuracy:* Fact-based inquiry that features listening to learn, the careful separation of facts and explanations, and respect for the power of story.
76– 100	*Authenticity:* Purpose-driven conversation that features respect for difference, the power of being for rather than against, and the discovery of intersections. Authenticity is the source of resilience, agility, and endurance in organizational life.

The higher the score on the meter, the lower the stress and supervision costs, the higher the commitment, and the better the results.

Below 50, we listen at the speed of opinion. Above 50, we listen at the speed of learning. The quality of listening drives the quality of speaking. If I am listening to avoid, that will generate pretense. If I'm listening for my own point of view, that will drive sincere, opinionated discussion. If I listen to learn by separating and researching facts and explanations, that spawns accurate inquiry. If I listen for purposes, contribution, and the intersection, that generates authenticity.

When we work with people to improve their communication, we ask them to embrace the "catch and correct" game. That is, to notice when they're below 50 on the meter, to take a breath, and to move up.

Here is how you move up the meter:

Moving up the Conversation Meter

CONVERSATION METER

	Focus: Listen to learn	**Ask questions**
Pretense *to* Sincerity	Research opinions, purposes, and concerns. • Ask questions they would like to answer. • Ask questions that can't be answered by "yes" or "no."	(Name), what is your opinion about (facts)? Have you seen a similar situation? Please tell me about that. What do you think we should do?
Sincerity *to* Accuracy	Research the facts and explanations. Uncover the facts behind the opinions.	Ask the reporter's questions: who, what, when, where, and how? • For example: What happened that has you say that? Are there any other possible explanations for those facts? Which explanation is most useful?
Accuracy *to* Authenticity	Research purpose.	For you, (Name), what is important about…? What makes that important to you? What are your essential purposes and concerns here? My sense of it is _____ is important to you, is that right?
Low-end Authenticity *to* High-end Authenticity	Research the intersection. Clarify essential purpose and reveal intersections for action.	If (X) is important to you and (Y) is important to me, how can we help one another? What do we have in common? What do you think is possible? What is it time for now?

More on using this meter is available online
at ***thevitalityimperative.com/explore***.

Here are a few ways to practice authenticity. Some are even entertaining!

Authenticity Practice #1: Chart a conversation

If you want a gripping short course in what obscures and frees the truth, watch *12 Angry Men*, a brilliant 1957 movie co-produced by Henry Fonda and directed by Sidney Lumet.

The movie centers on a murder trial. With a young man's life at stake, the jury of twelve votes 11 to 1 for conviction. Most are surprised that Juror No. 8, played by Fonda, doesn't go along.

"What do we do now?" says one juror. No. 8 responds, "I guess we talk." So, in a search for truth, they do.

At times, the way they talked decelerated the trip to truth, and other times the way they engaged quickened the trip. We think it is important to recognize the decelerators and the accelerators in conversations, and watching *12 Angry Men* will put you in the visceral presence of everything you just read and reflected on.

We think the movie presents a great, fun way to practice authenticity through the power of the Conversation Meter.

1. Print a Conversation Meter on paper big enough to write notes on. Go to ***thevitalityimperative.com/explore*** for a downloadable version of this tool.

2. Watch the movie and put check marks in the quadrant of the meter that fits the conversation on the screen.

3. At the end, count up how many examples of pretense, sincerity, accuracy, and authenticity you noted.

4. What did the quality of the conversation have to do with the story?

You can pick any movie or TV show and do the same chart-a-conversation exercise. Do it once a week for eight weeks, and you will have seared the elements of the meter into your consciousness forever.

If you are feeling bold, have someone you trust observe a real-life movie: one of your meetings! Have them chart the conversation on the meter, debrief with you, and discuss what there is to learn.

Authenticity Practice #2: From self-deceived to self-aware

The human mind is self-affirming. We tend to gather evidence for our own point of view and fail to notice when our own behavior is derailing the conversation. If you are up for elevating self-awareness, do the exercise below. As you become reliable for the following rhythm you will be able to lead others to do the same:

Notice your own sincere, strongly held opinion: Pick an opinion you know others around you do not all endorse.

- *Notice stress, and then breathe consciously.* To notice conversation stress, consider either of these signals:
  - When it feels like too much effort for too little impact, or
  - Resistance or disagreement is increasing with no improvement in sight.
  - Now breathe and note the shift from inhale to exhale. Relax your points of tension.
- *Notice your influence:* How are your thoughts, emotions, or physical signals contributing to the stress? Ask yourself and another person.
- *Make an opposite move:* Change a thought, emotion, or physical expression to its opposite. Some examples:
  - "He needs to change," to "I need to change my approach."
  - "Impatient anger" to "relaxed respect"
  - "Rolling my eyes" to "focused, interested eyes"
- *Notice the impact, and remember the lesson:* How was my mindset, emotions, or physical actions undermining my best interests? What new possibilities are emerging?

Authenticity is won, not simply desired. In the midst of life we are seduced, distracted, and sometimes confused. Are we learning to be true to ourselves? Are we true more often than not? It's a worthy fight.

Authenticity Practice #3: The Giraffe Award

An executive we admire told us about a monthly award at his company that we think is worth copying. It is called the Giraffe Award, and it honors those folks who stick their neck out. Once a month, the CEO personally acknowledges someone for having the courage and integrity to speak up about things that matter to the company, its purpose, and its culture.

What can you do to honor the people who stick their neck out? How could you institute a routine, signature action that promotes living in an honest, honorable community?

Here are some questions worth considering as you decide whether or not you want to promise Authenticity in your personal and professional life:

- Where is it important for me to be authentic?
- How do accurate, authentic conversations affect *community*?
- How do accurate, authentic conversations create opportunities for *contribution*?
- How do accurate, authentic conversations influence wholehearted *choice*?
- How can I develop more authenticity today? What, if anything, will I do differently?

For more on authenticity, including the resources and practices referenced in this chapter, go to ***thevitalityimperative.com/authenticity***.

•••

We have covered a lot thus far, all in the name of igniting the fire of vitality.

We have said that Vitality organizations and the people who work in them achieve more with less time, money, and stress.

We have said that the evidence of vitality is sustained business success accompanied by a common, three-part human experience: community, contribution, and choice.

We've also said that highly stressed organizations with poor results feature a different three-part experience: fear, mechanics, and manipulation.

And we've seen that leaders who reliably ignite vitality keep four important promises: (1) presence, (2) empathy, (3) purpose, and (4) authenticity.

And that leaders who reliably sustain vitality keep an additional three promises: (5) wonder, (6) timing, and (7) surprising results.

So, to sustain the journey, here comes an important but often overlooked fuel for the vitality fire: wonder.

PROMISE #5

WONDER:

Fueling the Future and Keeping Our Best Days in front of Us

Listen to anyone with an original idea, no matter how absurd it may sound at first. If you put fences around people, you get sheep. Give people the room they need.

—William L. McKnight, President, 3M

Being the richest man in the cemetery doesn't matter to me. . . . Going to bed at night saying we've done something wonderful . . . that's what matters to me.

—Steve Jobs

Anthropology demands the open-mindedness with which one must look and listen, record in astonishment and wonder that which one would not have been able to guess.

—Margaret Mead

"Well, we have an idea we'd like to run by you. We think the movie could be about a French gutter rat who wants to be a great chef . . . can we tell you more?"

How many people would have leaned forward, with curious regard, and said "Sure, tell me all about it." I mean, really, a rat? Nobody likes rats—especially in the kitchen!

When Jan Pinkava brought up the storyline to Pixar, however, Ed Catmull and John Lasseter listened. The animated movie *Ratatouille* went on to become an Academy Award-winning blockbuster that grossed more than $623 million.

Similarly, Pixar took a bet on a movie called *Wall-E*, a robot love story set in a trash-strewn apocalyptic future. What? Robots don't love! And, a trash dump . . . seriously? Even crazier, there wasn't even dialogue for the first half of the movie. Kids would never sit through it. Right?

Wrong. *Wall-E* also won an Academy Award and grossed over $521 million.

The first fourteen feature films released by Pixar won twelve Academy Awards and earned upwards of $8.5 billion worldwide. Clearly, Pixar is a success story worth wondering about.

Pixar Animation Studios was founded by Catmull and Alvy Ray Smith as a Steve-Jobs-funded spin-off from Lucasfilm. After early struggles, they enjoyed their first big success with *Toy Story* in 1995 and never looked back.

In his 2008 *HBR* article "How Pixar Fosters Collective Creativity," Catmull wrote, "The director and the other creative leaders of a production do not come up with all the ideas on their own; rather, every single member of the 200- to 250-person production group makes suggestions. Creativity must be present at every level of every artistic and technical part of the organization."

Without a doubt, all of us would like creativity to be present everywhere in our organizations, but how does that happen? Catmull noticed something important about Pixar's success: it was the result of talented people being smarter together than separately.

Catmull went on to show how organizational leaders can help develop this kind of culture.

What we can do is construct an environment that nurtures trusting and respectful relationships and unleashes everyone's creativity. If we get that right, the result is a vibrant community where talented people are loyal to one another and their collective work, everyone feels they are part of something extraordinary, and their passion and accomplishments make the community a magnet for talented people coming out of schools or working at other places. I know what I'm describing is the antithesis of the

free-agency practices that prevail in the movie industry, but that's the point: I believe
that community matters.

Pixar, 3M, Google, and other organizations with track records of innovation have learned that unprecedented brilliance arises far more reliably from a creative community than it does from ingenious individuals. This again is an example of the power of the Connected Leader model over the Superior Leader model of leadership. From our appreciative research into those and other innovative organizations, we have distilled the principles of wonder, as strange as that may sound.

How Does Wonder Produce More with Less?

Leaders who foster organizational wonder don't let probability destroy possibility. Indeed, wonder is the antidote to the ordinary. We are wise to nurture it because, otherwise, the past is as good as it gets. A leader who can promise wonder creates these benefits to community, contribution, and choice:

- *Wonder frees our natural desire to imagine* and breaks the grip of the past.
- *Wonder anticipates the future*, and that is a remarkable asset to managing risk. As we cultivate thinking from the future, we note opportunities and threats that many miss.
- *Wonder redeems mistakes*, making better use of resources, inspiring the dispirited, and leading to amazing things like penicillin, Velcro, Scotchgard, and Post-its.
- *Wonder creates options*, leading us to new and better choices.
- *Wonder sustains relationships*. When we've decided we're finished getting to know one another, our relationships begin, however slowly, to expire. Wonder keeps us interested, appreciative, and ready to be surprised by others—and even ourselves.
- *Wonder invigorates vitality*. Vitality can be ignited and, unfortunately, can be extinguished. Wonder combines curiosity and possibility to help us learn, grow, and contribute in the face of anything.

Wonder Principle #1: **People want to wonder**

Wonder is the capacity to be both awestruck by the present and imaginative about the future. Both are essential aspects of the antidote to ordinary. If you can't breathe possibility into today, you will stink at breathing it into tomorrow. The good news is that we are all naturally capable of awe and imagination.

Young people are overflowing with the qualities of wonder. Hunting for frogs becomes a grand expedition. Playing with cars becomes an epic, intergalactic race. A Lego set becomes a whole world unto itself.

On the journey to adulthood many of us lose touch with these birthright talents. The older we are, the more we need to know and control. Playful wonder is lost. It's silly. It's a waste of time. We forget that in not knowing, we gain curious presence, appreciation, and discovery that can never come from having all the answers.

Thankfully, the youthful traits of wonder can be preserved. Our bodies may age, but our minds can stay young as ever.

If you lived in Europe in the mid-sixteenth century, you might have experienced Commedia dell'Arte, the name given to the traveling troupes of actors who, with rough ideas and no scripts, entertained in town squares. In the twentieth century, a gifted teacher, Viola Spolin, built on that tradition and gave rise to what is now known as improvisational theater, or "improv." The famed Chicago theatrical troupe Second City, the long-running *Saturday Night Live,* and several generations of actors and directors all owe her great thanks. If the rest of us applied her lessons, we would also thank her.

In the 1940s, Spolin worked with aspiring child actors and discovered that her improvisational "theater games" relaxed stress and freed talent. When she applied the techniques with adults, the same thing happened. Actors including Mike Myers, Dan Aykroyd, Bill Murray, Tina Fey, Amy Poehler, Steve Carell, Julia Louis-Dreyfus, Ben Stiller, and Gilda Radner are proof of the approach. Spolin's students learned to be agile, collaborative, and creative in the face of unpredictability and surprise. Hey, maybe we could all use some of that!

What Spolin's work shows us is that wonder, when embraced, allows us to not fight against uncertainty, surprise, the unknown, and unpredictability, but instead to use it as a launching point for incredible creativity and innovation. We all have that capacity, and if we're honest with ourselves we all want to use it as often as possible.

After all, isn't awe of the present and imagination for the future a better place to be than stuck in cynicism and fear? (If you said, "No," please just put this book down and go chew on some lemons. You'll be happier.)

If you want to read about Spolin's remarkable work, check out *Improvisation for the Theater: A Handbook of Teaching and Directing Techniques*. You will learn more about coaching and teaching than comes with four years of graduate school. What follows is how we apply the improv approach to release the natural power of wonder.

Accessing Wonder: Presence, appreciation, and conversation

If you want to build more wonder into your life and into your organization, the good news is there are simple practices that we've already talked about in this book that can serve as the foundation for ever-increasing awe and imagination in every situation, no matter how difficult.

Presence
As you know, we think of presence as "awareness without prejudice." Wonder starts with connecting to what is right here and right now with relaxed awareness. The moment we introduce a regret about the past—a "should" about the present or a worry about the future—we dull our awareness and, in turn, limit our potential for intelligent response.

Appreciation
Just like a valuable investment appreciates over time, so can our connections with one another. The key is to listen for value and to curiously search for those things worthy of respect. When you listen for value, people feel safe. They are more likely to speak freely and creatively. When we listen for flaws, people feel blocked and are more likely to be careful than creative.

Conversation

When people disagree, they often don't converse. Instead, they compete and convince. When we converse, we learn and build. When we convince, we defend, attack, and seduce, which destroys the possibility of wonder.

In the authenticity chapter we introduced the Conversation Meter:

If you need to, go back and refresh your memory on this powerful communication tool. Above-50 conversations amplify wonder by allowing us to be candid and connected, to challenge and learn, and to combine and create.

When the challenges we face can't be met by what we already know or have already tried, it is time for wonder.

You can build wonder or block it. To build wonder, allow differences to provoke creativity. Different priorities (revenue growth versus cost reduction), competing demands (quarterly results versus long-term growth), different capabilities (marketing versus accounting), and different generations (baby boomers versus gen X and Y) all foster constructive, creative tension. Presence, appreciation, and conversation make it easier to reveal and learn from these differences, allowing new possibilities to emerge.

Wonder Principle #2: Differences + trust = brilliance

Being together does not mean being the same. In truth, collective creativity thrives on difference—as long as people believe in and trust one another.

Trust is essential for wonder to thrive. Have you ever seen great performance sustained over many years without the need for creativity? Pretty darn difficult. Have you ever attempted a creative breakthrough conversation with people you don't trust? Darn near impossible.

One of the most successful international sporting teams of all time comes from a country of 4.5 million people. Over the last hundred years they have won more than 75 percent of their matches and over 80 percent in the last ten years. In seven World Cup competitions, they have won twice, finished second once, and never finished lower than fourth against the top twenty teams in the world.

The sport is rugby, and the team is the New Zealand All Blacks. They are a splendid example of more with less because they compete and consistently win against many larger nations like England, France, Argentina, South Africa, Australia, United States, Japan, and Russia. They have built and preserved an extraordinary culture of trust through the three Vitality fundamentals of community, contribution, and choice. Please note how the All Blacks example might apply to your *vitality imperative*.

Trust and *Community*

Trust builds when a community features two things: common purpose, and having each other's backs.

The All Blacks are driven by the Maori tradition known as *whakapapa*, which includes deep regard for the layers of human history successive generations build upon. The Maori warrior history of humility and bravery is theirs to honor and to hand off to the next generation. Their famed *haka* dance, performed by the team before each contest, is a reminder of that lineage. They deeply believe that higher purpose delivers higher performance.

As a revered practice, the most senior members of the team sweep the locker room following matches. This act of humility is a reminder that no one is bigger than the collective community. Also, they value character over skill. Certainly high skill is a minimum qualification, but for the All Blacks it's not enough. The All Blacks want players who look out for one another and believe. To paraphrase Rudyard Kipling, the strength of the team is the player and the strength of the player is the team.

Trust and *Contribution*

The All Blacks have a saying, "Go for the gap." By this they mean you can always find something to improve, both as an individual and a team, no matter how successful you are. This passion for growing their contribution is a source of vitality, not fatigue.

Every member of the All Blacks promises to "leave the jersey in a better place." Every player develops a personal plan that includes specific goals for conditioning, nutrition, performance, and cultural fidelity. They measure progress, learn when they fall short, and celebrate when they succeed. Everyone knows where everyone else stands relative to his personal plan to contribute to the legacy of the jersey. This transparency about promises and progress strengthens trust between all the players and coaches. Without this mutual clarity and commitment, as the author Anne Lamott says, "Expectations are resentments under construction."

Trust and *Choice*

Sir Graham Henry, as coach of the All Blacks, led the team to eighty-eight victories in 103 matches. He knew a key to this record was the players participating in their own success and choosing to be extraordinary.

Henry said that, "Leadership groups were formed where seven players worked with coaches. While four players worked on tactics for the weekend game, three players would be working on team integration by sitting and eating together, and learning to respect and trust one another. Integrating team leaders was a key to the success of the team; some days the coaches ran training sessions and other days the team leaders took command."

Also, Henry observed, injuries decreased when players had the opportunity "to make choices and take decisions related to their training."

When the players felt trusted and relied upon, their performance improved and leadership emerged everywhere. This led to the All Blacks match-day mantra: "One captain, fifteen leaders."

Building this much trust shows up as sustained, creative accomplishment. For instance, shifting to the United States, if you study John Wooden's University of California, Los Angeles men's basketball program from 1948 to

1975, you will find they won ten NCAA championships in a twelve-year span at the end of his tenure. You will also find many examples of community, contribution, and choice. The New Zealand All Blacks, the UCLA Bruins, and other great legacies feature creativity that arises from those three foundational values, and this trust-built sense of wonder assures that these teams' best days are not behind them but always ahead.

Want to create these types of achievements in your organization? Release wonder, appreciate differences, build trust, and orchestrate diverse contributions. Give people a chance to be agents of collective success rather than victims of domination.

Wonder Principle #3: The past is information, not limitation

Many of our challenges demand that we move past probability into possibility. That leap calls for respecting the past without being restricted by it.

Paul Polman is the CEO of Unilever, the Dutch-British global consumer goods company. His early tenure was spent getting connected to the history of Unilever performance and of large organizational performance in general. He committed to a transparent environment so that many people had access to those facts and could co-create the future. Polman came to feel strongly that the success of Unilever, the health of our planet, and the health of society were interrelated. He believed that it was time to reinvent the nature of organizational growth.

After months of foraging through the facts of the past, the challenges of the present, and possibilities for the future, Polman developed a new purpose for Unilever: to double revenue while reducing environmental impact and improving social contributions around the world. Now that was a major wonder challenge—one that got people thinking, "I wonder how they are going to pull that off!"

Unilever has allowed this purpose to reveal competing tensions, provoke innovation, grow revenues, inspire employees, and build trust in their brands around the world. As we appreciate Unilever's achievements and those of other innovative organizations, we see a pattern of action worth considering:

preserve, eliminate, and create. In our work on releasing wonder, we've found that combining the three makes the past an asset rather than a hindrance.

Preserve: What will we carry forward?

Wonder is needed when major changes are afoot. To build the wonder, clarify what to preserve before you take on eliminate and create. When you clarify what to preserve, people have a stable place to stand to meet the creative challenges ahead. If everything looks like it is changing, people tend to be insecure, stressed, and terribly cautious.

Research the Past and Present through Both Accurate and Authentic Research

Accurate research confronts the facts, attractive or not, that deserve our attention. At Unilever, they confronted brand performance, growth trends, peer performance, and trends in consumer behavior and society at large. This allowed them to identify what they were doing well and what they needed to change with a clear and objective mindset.

Authentic research appreciates values, capabilities, contributions, and aspirations that are important to preserve. At Unilever, they researched the history of the company's character, even talking to retirees and long-time customers. They appreciated and summarized the ideals. They noticed that many of their biggest successes were meaningful, purpose-driven contributions for the people involved.

Allow Creative Tensions to Emerge

Start noticing conflicting priorities, demands, and options. These are conflicts between "right and right" rather than "right and wrong." As Polman writes in his book *Paradoxical Leadership to Enable Strategic Agility*, "The difference between average and outstanding firms is an 'AND Mentality.' We must find and create tensions—force people into different space for thinking. . . . This is not just a performance issue but a survival issue, because managing paradox helps foster creativity and high performance." In their work at Unilever, Polman and his colleagues named things like short-term versus long-term results, growing the business versus decreasing environmental impact, and return to shareholders versus contribution to society as the key creative tensions for growth.

Reveal a Guiding Purpose

Research and creative tension are important, but they must also be in service to a common purpose, which becomes the framework for interpretation of your findings and discussions. There are some important questions that must be asked in determining this guiding purpose. Standing in the fruits of the research, ask and answer:

- What is important to the people we serve?
- What do we have to give?
- What would we love to give?
- What competing tensions do we face?
- What purpose includes and respects all of that?

At Unilever, the guiding purposes became:

- *We work to create a better future every day.*
- *We help people feel good, look good, and get more out of life with brands and service that are good for them and good for others.*
- *We will inspire people to take small, everyday actions that can add up to a big difference in the world.*
- *We will develop new ways of doing business with the aim of doubling the size of our company while reducing environmental impact.*

Be True to the Purpose

Finally, decide what you will preserve from the past and what you will carry into the future. At Unilever, they spoke of the difference between their values that had founded the company, which they were honoring and preserving, and the execution culture, which needed to change. All the change priorities would be true to their values.

Eliminate: Stop off-purpose activity

Once you have determined what to preserve in your organization, it is then time to aggressively pursue what needs to be eliminated in order to ensure the guiding purpose is honored and accomplished. This can be a combination of practices, systems, traditions, and staffing.

As you do this, keep purpose present. Behavior is correlated to awareness. If we want new behavior, we need new, reliable awareness of the purpose.

Ask yourself: what is clearly off-purpose? What do we know must stop? How and when will we stop it? What routines will keep us from noticing and eliminating off-purpose activity?

Without the courage to stop, pull off the bandage, and discard what has become off-purpose, resources are wasted, complacency goes up, and creative fire goes down.

At Unilever, executive positions were eliminated, businesses were sold, and elements of the organizational structure were removed—all in service to the guiding purpose. When this was accomplished, and the reasons were clearly explained, an amazing thing happened: employees were energized and innovation happened at an accelerated rate. There was a clear path forward.

Create: Think from the future to meet the challenges of today

At Unilever, wondering about tensions has generated many inspiring, effective ideas. For examples, you can go to YouTube and search the "Dove beauty ads." Many find the videos deeply moving. Here is what is unarguable: in 2013, Dove's "Real Beauty Sketches" ad became one of the most watched video ads of all time.

Wonder loves paradox. Experiment with your *vitality imperative*. What creative tensions are relevant to your purpose? Pick one, like Unilever's "return to shareholders" versus "making a contribution to society."

Then, ask, "How does each extreme contribute to our purpose? How does each extreme hurt our purpose?"

Questions build or block wonder. We have noted that the questions that build wonder increase interest and energy. The ones that block and even destroy wonder turn people into impotent critics. Energizing questions tend to have three attractions:

- *Rational:* People think, "That's a smart question!"
- *Emotional:* People feel, "I care about this!"
- *Physical:* People lean forward and start talking, e.g., "How can our marketing budget touch and inspire people around the world?"

We believe deeply that purpose + paradox = wonder. If you are interested in going more deeply into the high-value challenge of competing tensions, we recommend reading *The Unfinished Leader: Balancing Contradictory Answers to Unsolvable Problems,* by David Dotlich, Peter Cairo, and Cade Cowan. We love the title because the need for wonder, to borrow from Eric Hoffer, is "perpetually unfinished."

Wonder Principle #4: New connections create new possibilities

Author Stephen Johnson says, "The lone genius is kind of a myth and almost every innovation comes out of a kind of a collaborative network." This leads to a simple truth: If we continually refresh our network of connections, we will continually refresh wonder.

Here's a question to ponder: How can winemaking lead to better vision for millions of people?

In the fifteenth century, Johannes Gutenberg famously saw a possible connection between the grape presses used in winemaking and a coin stamp. That insight led to the printing press and movable type. In *How We Got to Now: Six Innovations That Changed the Modern World,* Johnson writes about how the resulting printed books revealed a problem: many people were too farsighted to read. For years, aging monks reading manuscripts had known that placing glass over pages and holding that glass at the right angle made the print easier to read. With books becoming available to larger populations, making them easier to read was in demand, and that demand led to experimentation with glass. This led to the creation of spectacles, eyeglasses, telescopes, and more. That's worth raising a glass of wine to.

If you want surprising, relevant contributions coming from your organization, experiment with new connections.

At places like Google, Apple, 3M, and, most recently, Microsoft, physical spaces are designed to cause surprising connections. For instance, very different functions share the same refreshment areas and restrooms, resulting in unexpected conversations.

Personally, you can do a job you do not normally do. Thodey and fellow executives at Telstra working in a call center or Adam Lowry and executives at Method Home staffing the reception desk are good examples.

Talk to customers and colleagues you do not normally contact. Learn something new in each conversation. Ask thought-provoking questions, like:

- "In your work, what is impossible that you wish were possible?"
- "What have you learned recently?"
- "For you, what people or experiences have been unusually valuable?"
- "What questions would you really like to answer?"

In his book *Against the Gods: The Remarkable Story of Risk*, Peter Bernstein writes that Marin Mersenne was "the center of the world of science and mathematics during the first half of the 1600s." While a formidable intellect himself, Mersenne's major contribution was connection. He was a theologian, mathematician, music theorist, and philosopher who functioned in the math and science community as "the post box of Europe." Mersenne knew Galileo, Descartes, Pascal, Torricelli, and many others. He connected them to each other and others to them. Innovations like vacuum technology, barometric pressure, and the barometer itself ensued.

As a leader, whom can you connect? What wonders will come out of it?

Wonder Principle #5: Wonder thrives on appreciation

Appreciation is the antidote to pessimism. If you want to break the grip of gloom, find something to admire.

Don Shula is the winningest head coach in the history of the National Football League. He did a brilliant job of achieving more with less. As coach of the Miami Dolphins, he won the Super Bowl twice and appeared in the big game three other times. His 1972 Dolphins remain the only undefeated team in the history of the NFL. That team featured a defensive unit called the No-Name Defense because of the lack of famous players. Fellow coach O.A. "Bum" Phillips said that Shula was the only coach he knew who could take his team and beat yours, and then take your team and beat his.

Shula was brilliant at appreciating and orchestrating the strengths of players, constantly wondering about how their various strengths complemented one another. As he recognized underappreciated merits, the players themselves began to wonder what might be possible about their own performance. They tried harder. They played better.

Many leaders focus more on correcting flaws rather than revealing, developing, and reallocating strengths. Revealing strengths that most leaders miss requires observing in ways most leaders don't.

Most leaders practice reactive appreciation, which is thoughtless, impulsive affection. Thoughtless appreciation tends to be limited to things like what one already likes. People and things that are unlike what one already enjoys tend to trigger more distaste than appreciation. They might as well wear a sign on their foreheads that says, "No new discoveries here."

Rare leaders, however, are good at proactive appreciation, which is thoughtful, purposeful discovery of things to admire—looking and listening for value rather than quickly labeling something as valuable or not. Practice proactive appreciation and the limits of your own thinking fall away. Wonder grows and new ideas emerge.

Here are a few exercises to get you started.

- Think of someone close to you whom you admire. Note five things you appreciate. When you are in the presence of someone you appreciate, does your mind open or close to new possibilities?

- Think of someone in your life you have not appreciated. Find five things about him or her you respect or admire. Do not stop until you see five things genuinely worthy of your regard. Is your mind opening to new possibilities or closing down further?

- Right now, wherever you are, stop, take a breath, and find five things to appreciate. Perhaps a useful design element of the room or a tool, enjoyable textures or colors, interesting plants or animals. Take a moment to enjoy each of the five. Is your mind opening or closing?

G.K. Chesterton said, "We are perishing for want of wonder, not for want of wonders." Appreciation is not mere reaction. It's a skill to cultivate. Practice seeing the extraordinary in the ordinary. Go do something you have never done and appreciate something new. Beauty and laughter are friends to wonder, so enjoy new beauty and laugh at new things. When we do so, limitations dissolve, and wonder runs free.

Now, here are a few ways to cultivate wonder.

Wonder Practice #1: "No, but" versus "Yes, and"

If you were to interview comedians at *Whose Line Is It Anyway?*, Second City, or *Saturday Night Live*, you would find they all revere the importance of "Yes, and." Try the following experiment, and you'll see why.

Gather a small group of people (three to eight) who have any circumstance in common. Tell them you are asking them to have two rounds of discussions about the same topic. In both cases, the discussion starts by someone saying a single sentence about their common circumstance. For example, "We are behind schedule on the cost-reduction program."

- *First round:* After the first sentence, each person says, "No, but" and then adds a sentence. Moving quickly, go around the group twice.

- *Second round:* After the first sentence, each person says, "Yes, and" and then adds a sentence.

Once the discussions are complete, ask the group what was different between "No, but" and "Yes, and."

In the many times we've done this, people report that the first pass slowed thinking, increased tension, and blocked creative ideas. The second pass was faster, more creative, and built on one another's comments.

Practicing "but" versus "and" tends to refresh wonder and, in turn, our natural desire to build rather than destroy.

Wonder Practice #2: Anticipation

Humans are good at imagining the future, and there are practical ways to put that ability to work. The following two-part exercise can make a valuable difference. It starts by identifying an important goal and gathering the group of people who are critical to success. After clarifying the goal, ask those people to imagine two futures: failure and success.

Wonder about Failure
Imagine it is one year from today (or whatever time fits your important goal) and we have failed. What are the three to five mistakes that explain our failure? Have people answer individually, and then gather the answers. What themes do you see?

Wonder about Success
Imagine it is one year from today and we have succeeded and exceeded our own expectations. What three to five ingredients explain our success? Have people answer individually, and then gather the answers. What themes do you see?

Insights and Implications
What useful insights do you find? What are the implications for new action? What actions will we take now?

Wonder Practice #3: Look for surprise

Few people go looking for surprise, but when you do, it produces surprising and relevant results. When Procter & Gamble took a fresh look at a long-time product, Pampers, they found an unappreciated contribution: babies slept more quickly and more soundly in Pampers than in cloth diapers. That surprise led to a whole new reason to buy an already-developed product, and sales soared. What surprises lie hidden around you? Try these kinds of surprise research to find out.

A Network of Relationship: Who wins when we win?

Find a few people in your organization who are interested in revealing surprising, underappreciated relationships. Think of a big recent success relative to your work, one you would love to clone. Then do the following activity:

- On a large space (e.g., whiteboard) write the names of clients and colleagues who were core to the effort.
- For twenty minutes, ask and answer, "Who benefited from our success?"
- Write the new names on the board and draw lines to show how they are connected to others on the board. Who could benefit from our success but hasn't yet?
- What surprises you? What are the implications? What actions are you eager to take?

A Surprise Survey: What surprised you recently?

Host a week-long research project. Get ready to capture surprises in whatever way is easiest for you (e.g., tablet, journal, smartphone, recording app, etc.).

Every day, ask five different people, "What surprised you recently?"

- Note their answers.
- Note any moments when you are surprised by their answers.
- Note any other surprises you experience that week.
- At the end of the week, review your journal of surprise. What did you learn? What insights were there? New possibilities? Do you have any actions to take?

I wonder what difference you can make if you promise to cultivate an environment where you and others are free to wonder? Will you?

Here are some questions worth considering as you decide whether or not you want to promise wonder in your personal and professional life:

- Where is it important for me to strengthen wonder and be open to new possibilities?
- How does a sense of wonder improve *community*?
- How does a sense of wonder improve *contribution*?
- How does a sense of wonder inspire *choice*?
- How can I develop more wonder today? What, if anything, will I do differently?

For more on wonder, including materials and practices referenced above, go to ***thevitalityimperative.com/wonder***.

PROMISE #6

TIMING:

The Victory of Evolution over Revolution

You don't have to swing hard to hit a home run.
If you've got the timing, it'll go.

—Yogi Berra

Our industry does not respect tradition.
It only respects innovation.

—Satya Nadella, CEO, Microsoft

You just have to use your time where it's most critical.

—Julia Newton-Howes, CEO of CARE Australia

On May 20, 2012, devastating earthquakes struck the Emilia-Romagna region of Italy. The means of production for two important products from the region, rice and Parmigiano Reggiano, were badly damaged, as were many of the places where those products were stored, including nearly half of the annual production of the cheese, some 360,000 big wheels. A representative of the main Parmigiano Reggiano consortium went to Modena to see Massimo Bottura, one of the top restauranteurs in the world.

"Massimo, you have to help us. This is a disaster!" the representative said. "If we don't act very quickly everyone goes out of business, and we lose everything!"

Bottura considered the elements of the challenge: damaged cheese and rice, which must be used quickly or be lost; a famous culinary region in peril;

global press coverage; and ease of connection to people around the world via the Internet and social media. He went back to the president of the consortium and said, "I have the idea!"

Bottura's idea was to recreate a famed Roman pasta dish known as *cacio e pepe* (cheese and pepper) and substitute rice for the pasta and Parmigiano Reggiano for the traditional Pecorino Romano cheese. "I wanted to create a dinner anyone in the world could cook, show everyone what had happened in Modena, and show them what they can do. In Japan, London, New York, everywhere they were cooking *risotto cacio e pepe*. Forty thousand people were cooking, and all 360,000 wheels sold out. No one lost a job. No one closed their doors."

Bottura started with an iconic Italian pasta dish and, as he describes it, "transformed it into an Emilian symbol of hope and recovery by using Parmigiano instead of Pecorino and rice instead of pasta." The timing was perfect.

Bottura is an artist of evolution who has brought classic Italian cuisine into a new era of creativity. Some even refer to his cooking as revolutionary, although by our definition of revolution, we do not. In speaking about organizational leadership, here is what we mean by these terms:

- *Evolution:* Building on the value of the past, and responding well to fresh challenges and opportunities to create new value. The leader's contribution to high-value evolution is great timing through preserved purpose and accelerated progress.

- *Revolution:* Abrupt overthrow of the past featuring blame of the villains and installation of new saviors. The villains had bad timing. The new saviors now have a chance to reinvent the entire system.

In a given moment we can always do something, but we cannot do everything. The better our actions fit the moment, the more results we produce per unit of time, money, and stress. However, there are many examples of otherwise intelligent, successful leaders with terrible timing—and the organizational costs are high.

Continually missing the right moment leaves huge piles of unresolved issues. Finally, stakeholder patience runs out, and the revolution begins: leaders are tossed, people lose their jobs, programs are canceled, and organizational structure and process go through radical, wrenching change.

Oh, and change consultants get paid millions of unnecessary dollars.

How Does Timing Produce More with Less?

Revolution is an act of desperation for organizations incompetent at evolution. All over the world, hundreds of millions of dollars are wasted on huge change management projects that are only necessary because of a failure to evolve. A great sense of timing is a leader's contribution to an agile, ever-evolving enterprise—and the return on investment can be staggering.

A leader who can keep the timing promise creates massive value. Timing contributes to community, contribution, and choice by:

- *Improving leverage*, getting more out of time, money, and talent.
- *Reducing resistance and increasing alignment.* Has someone raised an issue with you that did not fit what mattered at the moment? Did you resist? When the issue is timely, then interest and cooperation soar.
- *Accelerating achievement* as resistance is replaced by focused, dedicated action.
- *Increasing the credibility of leadership* as avoidance is replaced with brave, realistic action.
- *Increasing the joy of work and the honor of belonging* because it is deeply satisfying to get more done per unit of time, money, and stress.

So, what is it time for now? The principles of timing, of course!

Timing Principle #1: Beware the timing traps!

One of the best-known experiments in the history of psychology is featured in Christopher Chabris and Daniel Simons' book *The Invisible Gorilla: And Other Ways Our Intuitions Deceive Us*. Simons describes the experiment:

Imagine you are asked to watch a short video in which six people—three in white shirts and three in black shirts—pass basketballs around. While you watch, you must keep a silent count of the number of passes made by the people in white shirts. At some point, a gorilla strolls into the middle of the action, faces the camera and thumps its chest, and then leaves, spending nine seconds on screen. Would you see the gorilla?

Almost everyone has the intuition that the answer is, "Yes, of course I would." How could something so obvious go completely unnoticed? But when we did this experiment at Harvard University several years ago, we found that half of the people who watched the video and counted the passes missed the gorilla. It was as though the gorilla was invisible.

Try showing the video (available through ***thevitalityimperative.com/ explore***) to people who have not heard of the experiment, and ask them to keep silent count of the passes made by people in white shirts. The results are fascinating.

The issue of selective attention is important to great timing. In two of his books, *Attention and Effort* and *Thinking, Fast and Slow,* Nobel Prize-winning psychologist Daniel Kahneman shows that locking our attention on one thing can obscure other observations. In our work with organizations, we have found predictable areas of accidental attention that act as wasteful time traps both for leaders and the organizations as a whole.

The first five Vitality promises—presence, empathy, purpose, authenticity, and wonder—build the foundation for great timing. This brings up an important truth: the Vitality promises are interrelated. They are a package deal. If one promise is broken, it compromises all the other promises. If you find that you are running into roadblocks in trying to achieve your *vitality imperative*, take inventory of yourself, your team, and then your organization to see where you might be breaking your Vitality promises. The timing traps are a great example of how we violate those promises, and each one is a surefire way to miss the moment.

The Anti-Presence Trap: "This shouldn't be happening!"

When our attention is riveted on distress over what is happening rather than acknowledging current realities with a mindset of leaving things better than we found them, stress increases and timing suffers. Recent research confirms this:

In her TED Talk, Stanford University psychologist Kelly McGonigal states that throughout her career she has advised her patients to rid stress from their lives because it can have a negative impact on the human body—she has made stress the 'enemy'. However, recent work by Lauren Wisk, PhD, and her colleagues has her revising her approach to stress.

Described in a 2011 American Psychological Association article, Dr. Wisk's team linked survey data on nearly 30,000 U.S. adults to national death records in order to determine the relationship between levels of stress, the perception that stress impacts health and health outcomes. They found that both higher levels of reported stress and the perception that stress affects health were independently associated with worse physical and mental health.

Most strikingly, those who reported a lot of stress and that stress greatly impacted their health together had a 43 percent increased risk of premature death (over an eight-year period), suggesting that how you think about stress matters just as much as how much stress you have.

When you change your mind about stress you can change your body's response to stress. The presenter suggests that when stress is viewed as a positive, something helpful to performance, a person will be able to decrease the negative effects of stress on physical health.

Relating to what *is* happening as though it *shouldn't be* happening is a strange and yet popular form of denial—and it's wickedly bad for health and timing.

The Anti-Empathy Trap: Disapproval, prejudice, and suppression

An essential key to managing risk is the free flow of information: the better the information, the lower the risk, and timely opportunity becomes clear. Through misuse of power, however, leaders can destroy the free flow of information. With power can come hubris, and hubris is prone to irrational and rapid disapproval.

A powerful, financially successful executive was the president of a business unit headquartered in London. His business decisions had produced high profits and as the profits increased, so did his autonomy. However, he was irrationally certain of his own view and disapproved of dissent.

He became known for intolerance, belittling colleagues, and criticizing dissenters as weak and stupid. His adamant certainty and volatile disapproval suppressed relevant information and healthy debate. Mere months after he publicly assured investors that risks were slight and the future was bright, disaster struck.

This executive's name is Joe Cassano, and his business unit, AIG Financial Products, collapsed. His now-legendary credit default swap contracts became exposed as high-risk and underfunded. Many researchers now think that Cassano and the AIG Financial Products strategies were significant contributors to the the Great Recession of 2008. To this day, Cassano denies any personal culpability for what became the largest government bailout of a private company in U.S. history.

Primatologist Jane Goodall once wisely said, "Change happens by listening and then starting a dialogue with the people who are doing something you don't believe is right." That requires empathy. When leaders like Cassano disapprove of and diminish competing views, the intelligence of the enterprise declines. Dissent is suppressed, risk goes up, and timing goes down (and sometimes global economies, too).

The Anti-Purpose Trap: Results without reason

Focusing on results is good, right? Yes, *if* the results are connected to a purpose. A purpose is the reason we exist, and that reason should have a longer shelf life than current methods and results. Said another way, who we are endures longer than what we do.

Many people explain Blockbuster's failure in one word: Netflix. That, however, is misleading. At one point Netflix was struggling so much that it offered itself for sale to Blockbuster for a modest $20 million. Blockbuster declined, and the reason for that decision has much to do with Blockbuster's demise.

When Wayne Huizenga purchased the then-small video store chain in 1987 he believed its purpose to be entertainment, not simply video rentals. Who we *are* is entertainment and what we currently *do* is rent videos. That view was ratified when Viacom, an entertainment conglomerate, purchased Blockbuster in 1994 for over $18 billion. However, several CEOs later Blockbuster was operating only as a retail company, the original purpose was no longer guiding decision making and retail profit was all that mattered. If the purpose is entertainment, then the Netflix deal seems apt; if all that matters is retail store profits then it seems off course. What seemed on-course? Continuing to milk consumers for the highly profitable and unpopular late fees. That purposeless addiction to the retail store result delayed Blockbuster's response to Netflix sending videos through the mail, cable, and phone companies offering video-on-demand, and Redbox renting videos through vending machines for one dollar. As one business pundit said when the slow-to-react company became defunct, "Blockbuster paid the ultimate late fee."

The Anti-Authenticity Trap: False positive leadership

A "false positive" is when a condition is observed to be present when in fact the indicators were misleading and it isn't. Many leaders avoid bad news and unwelcome information, thinking it is their job to "be positive." As former President John Adams once said, "Facts are stubborn things; and whatever may be our wishes, our inclinations, or the dictates of our passions, they cannot alter the state of facts and evidence."

As Toyota began to make inroads into General Motors' global auto manufacturing leadership, Roger Smith, then GM's CEO, assured people that the car manufacturer was still the best auto company in the world. Their only challenge, said Smith, was "costly and unnecessary government regulation." A falsely positive assurance in the face of declining results and seismic industry changes was costly. In 2009, GM went bankrupt and was saved only by a $50-billion government bailout.

After decades of massive success, Firestone was challenged by Michelin's introduction of radial tires, which lasted twice as long as Firestone's bias tires, into the United States. Consumers flocked to the new option. Many in Firestone had sounded the warning bells about the evolution in tire design, and yet, Firestone was late and slow to react.

After finally investing in the new technology, Firestone ignored again the fact that radials lasted longer, and so overall tire consumption was destined to fall. Firestone remained falsely positive, even renting warehouses to store unsold tires for the time when consumption would rise again. That fantasy never came to pass, expense cuts led to quality problems, and Firestone was ultimately sold to Bridgestone.

Authentic optimism embraces reality. The falsely positive leader is afflicted with one or both of two ailments: self-deception and mistrust in the resilient, resourceful creativity of colleagues.

The Anti-Wonder Trap: Addiction to past glory

Kodak built a brilliant business, holding more than 90 percent of the U.S. film market and 85 percent of camera sales. Loyal consumers were out looking for their own "Kodak moment" and profitable revenue was high. The popular story is that Kodak was blindsided by a new technology: digital photography. In fact, Kodak engineer Steven Sasson invented the first digital camera in 1975. Instead of commercializing this breakthrough technology, however, Kodak executives chose to keep the development quiet so as not to compete with their high-profit film business. Protecting their historical cash flow was more important than technological trends and customer value. That false choice obscured a timely question: "How do we keep the lion's share of the film market on our way to dominating digital?" That would have been worth wondering.

As digital photography emerged in the marketplace, Kodak's response was to increase marketing to halt consumer trends. By the time Kodak surrendered to digital reality, it was too late. When we only protect the past, we stop wondering about the future.

Embrace the Vitality promises to avoid the timing traps. Great timing welcomes the present, empathizes with difference, preserves purpose, confronts the truth, and wonders about progress.

Timing Principle #2: Align deeply, act quickly, and adjust often

All over the world, across industries and cultures, we have found that sustained success features a repeating cycle:

Leaders who respect that rhythm find that their ability to do three monumentally important things soars:

- *Diagnose:* Understand the reason why a problem or opportunity exists.
- *Predict:* See the impending results before they actually happen.
- *Prescribe:* Identify and implement the actions it is time for now.

Please keep your *vitality imperative* in mind. Later in this chapter we will give you a simple set of questions that allow you to diagnose the situation, predict the future, and prescribe timely action.

We've found that few leaders adhere to the rhythm of the timing cycle. We think that is one reason why Deloitte's Shift Index shows that the average life expectancy of a Fortune 500 company has declined from around seventy-five years half a century ago to fewer than fifteen years today, and is trending toward five years.

It is easy to find examples of companies who failed or continue to fail at aligning deeply, acting quickly, and adjusting often. BlackBerry, Borders, and many others come to mind. It is useful, though, to appreciate an organization that has great timing and to see what we can learn from their success.

In 2010, four people who met at the Wharton School of the University of Pennsylvania launched a company. Neil Blumenthal, Andrew Hunt, David Gilboa, and Jeffrey Raider saw a problem they wanted to solve, and they have done it well. That enterprise, Warby Parker, launched with a $2,500 seed investment, is now valued at $1.2 billion. *Fast Company* recently named the company the most innovative company of 2015. Let's map Warby Parker's success against the timing cycle and see what organizations large and small can learn.

Align: Gathering stakeholders and resources in support of the contribution you are trying to make

The legitimate reason for an enterprise is contribution. The reason to create an organization is to make a better contribution than you could make on your own. Often that begins with a problem to solve.

From the Warby Parker website:

> *Every idea starts with a problem. Ours was simple: glasses are too expensive. We were students when one of us lost his glasses on a backpacking trip. The cost of replacing them was so high that he spent the first semester of grad school without them, squinting and complaining. (We don't recommend this.) The rest of us had similar experiences, and we were amazed at how hard it was to find a pair of great frames that didn't leave our wallets bare.*

As Blumenthal told *Fast Company*, "It didn't make sense to us that a pair of eyeglasses should cost as much or more than an iPhone."

Align conversations answer three questions: (1) intersect, (2) invent, and (3) invest.

Align Question #1: Intersect. Do we have a clear contribution that is supported by data and attractive to stakeholders? What contribution is at the intersection?

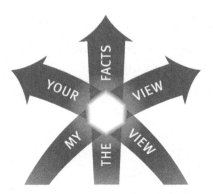

As we mentioned in the authenticity promise, the Conversation Meter helps reveal the intersection:

The Warby Parker journey began with a sincere complaint: "Glasses are too expensive!" A vital contribution, however, needs to be accurate (fact-based) and authentic (purpose-driven). By practicing accuracy, the Warby Parker discovered these relevant facts and valuable explanations:

- *Fact:* The eyeglass industry is dominated by a single global player. Luxottica is the world's largest eyewear company, controlling more than 80 percent of the world's major eyewear brands such as Ray-Ban, Persol, and Oakley, and retailers including LensCrafters, Pearle Vision, Sears Optical, Target Optical, EyeMed Vision Care, and Glasses.com.

- *Explanation:* Any market dominated by a single player tends to have high margins and low customer service. We could make a difference!

After practicing accuracy, the Warby Parker team held authentic conversations that revealed relevant stakeholders and valuable contribution:

- *Stakeholders:* "We know we need to create shareholder value, and we think serving these stakeholders is the way to do it," said Blumenthal.

- *Customers:* "Treat customers the way we'd like to be treated. They don't call it the golden rule for nothing."

- *Employees:* "Create an environment where employees can think big, have fun, and do good."

- *Community:* "Get out there. No company is an island. Serving the community is in our DNA."

- *Environment:* "Green is good. Warby Parker is one of the only carbon-neutral eyewear brands in the world."

- *Contribution:* From the Warby Parker website, "Warby Parker was founded with a rebellious spirit and a lofty objective: to offer designer eyewear at a revolutionary price, while leading the way for socially conscious businesses." The founders believe that their objective intersects with the conditions in the marketplace and the best interests of the stakeholders they promised to serve.

Intersect conversations are candid and curious. They are voyages of discovery rather than battles over who is right. Make it safe to express and learn from diverse views on your way to the intersection.

Align Question #2: Invent. Do we have enough creative solutions to achieve our purpose?

The intelligent, informed, and playful people of Warby Parker keep developing and experimenting with creative solutions, like:

- Software that lets a customer upload a picture of themselves and then see various frames on their own face.

- A Home Try-On program: free shipping for a five-frame kit so customers can try frames in the privacy of their homes.

- Thirty-seconds-or-less videos that answer frequent customer questions and that can be easily attached in a Twitter conversation.

- Giving a pair of glasses to those in need for every pair purchased.

The spirit of playful wonder is chronic at Warby Parker. They have built a culture rich in customer empathy, always alert to the customer experience. Everyone is asked to contribute weekly innovation ideas. Says Blumenthal, "We think a lot about being a disruptive company. The question is, how do you remain a disruptive company? How do you create a culture of innovation? The first way is actually asking for innovation." As they keep asking, the ideas keep coming.

Invent conversations are bold and provocative. Test ideas, build on ideas, and challenge ideas in a mood of eager, interested discovery.

Align Question #3: Invest. Have we allocated time, money, and talent to achieve our objectives?

When there are many good ideas on the table, the challenge is deciding where to allocate resources. In any organization, resource conflicts abound. How do you best resolve them? As Blumenthal says, "Our customers, employees, community, and environment are our stakeholders. We consider them in every decision we make."

Decision criteria are hugely valuable because people learn to argue against the criteria rather than against one another. That leads to open, healthy debate.

At Warby Parker, the always-on criterion is the lofty objective of the company—to offer designer eyewear at a revolutionary price, while leading the way for socially conscious businesses. Moreover, the objective serves the interests of the four stakeholders: customers, employees, community, and environment.

Many leaders confuse agreement with alignment. Agreement is mutual approval of an idea. Alignment, however, moves beyond agreement, requiring allocation of sufficient time, money, and talent to execute. Agreement is conceptual; alignment confronts reality. By testing ideas against agreed-upon criteria, Warby Parker works through questions and conflicts in order to align resources with strategy. For example, the seconds-long customer-response videos were enormously popular with customers, employees, and community members. So, they increased investment, and there are now over two thousand of those short videos.

The deadly mistake leaders often make is to avoid confronting resource allocation conflicts, opting instead for fake alignment. Invest conversations recognize, raise, and resolve conflicts rather than avoiding them.

The work of alignment takes patience, and those eager to act without true alignment can sell that work short. Intersecting with conditions and stakeholders is crucial research. An exciting idea lacking that research can crash and burn because conditions and relationships do not support success. The desire to invest wanes, and the idea fails for lack of support, à la Groupon, Webvan, and Pets.com.

Act: Providing the information and clarity people need in order to execute

Action without alignment is a misguided gamble. Alignment without action is self-indulgent waste. When it is time to act three questions matter: (1) engage, (2) clarify, and (3) close.

Act Question #1: Engage. Do the people who will get it done understand and authentically support the purpose and plan?

Warby Parker is a high-transparency environment. People who do the work are involved in creating the plans and in explaining the why, how, and what to new arrivals. "One of the promises we make to employees is that there are never any surprises," says Blumenthal. Plans are fact-based, purpose-driven, and understood by all. Weekly company-wide meetings keep people connected to everything that is going on.

Act Question #2: Clarify. Who is promising to do what and by when?

At Warby Parker, accountabilities are clear, public, and tracked. No misunderstanding, no mischief. Everyone knows who promises what and the state of performance.

Act Question #3: Close. Are people personally committed and producing results?

Warby Parker's founders' commitment to "create an environment where employees can think big, have fun and do good," means hiring people who want to be there. That sense of choice extends to specific roles and, every week, employees are asked to rate their on-the-job happiness on a scale of one to ten and explain their rating. This frequent check gives leaders early alerts to disruptions in personal commitment and performance.

Once people commit, help them take the first successful action. Get them going quickly, and then adjust often.

Adjust: turning experience into improvement

Great timing is not about perfection—it's about correction.

One reason small organizations like Warby Parker, Method Home, and Zappos can go from zero to wonderful so quickly is their rate of adjustment. As some large companies have found out the hard way, rate of adjustment can beat economies of scale.

Adjust conversations answer two questions: (1) review and (2) renew.

Adjust Question #1: Review. Do our metrics help us learn and improve?

One of the three governors of Vitality is the spirit of contribution: people love making a measurable difference. Great metrics give real-time evidence of contribution and inspire improvement.

Warby Parker's Director of Data Science Carl Anderson says, "Our data dictionary is hugely valuable. Prior to its existence, we had no assurance that analysts on different teams were using the same definitions to define metrics and, even when metrics were defined, we had nowhere to document them. Now, everybody speaks the same language. Developing this source of truth was a long endeavor." The Data Book, as it's called, is continually updated and metrics like "net promoter score" (a measure of customer loyalty and enthusiasm) are known by all. It has become wildly popular and widely used.

When metrics are tied to contribution they become embraced. Accountability is based on the drive to make a difference rather than avoiding shame and blame. Informal conversations about "how we are doing" expand and those informal conversations produce way more improvement than formal reviews. When the mood is *for contribution* rather than *against failure* results are even better.

Adjust Question #2: Renew. Do we have effective routines for identifying and making smart changes?

From *Business Insider*:

> *Blumenthal says that every month the four founders return to the bar where they originally came up with the idea, and one of them is placed in the hot seat. According to Blumenthal, during these "360 reviews," a partner might say, "When you shoot me a ten-page email at two in the morning, I want to punch you in the face."*
>
> *"That set the tone for the culture at Warby Parker, which would really be rooted in open and honest feedback," says Blumenthal.*
>
> *This culture of communication isn't reserved only for the founders. The entire Warby Parker staff is given a 360 review every quarter. Although this takes up a lot of time, Blumenthal says, "as a manager, it's your highest priority to be developing your people." And employees should never be surprised by how they're doing work-wise, he says.*

Timing soars when we:

- *Align deeply:* Step over no relevant conflict.
- *Act quickly:* Take action and learn rather than delay while we prepare perfectly.
- *Adjust often:* Measure contribution, learn from success and shortfall, and help people make a valuable difference.

Timing Principle #3: Above all, love the question, "What is it time for now?"

Some questions are asked, answered, and done with, such as, "What were our revenues last month?" Some questions, though, are worth asking over and over and never to be done with, like the timing question: "What is it time for *now*?"

Keeping the timing question alive changes what we see and do in two domains:

- *The content of the conversation:* What subject deserves attention now? What may be important and is still not the best use of this moment? What is at the intersection of our interests, the interests of stakeholders, and the circumstances we share?

- *The quality of the conversation:* It is always time for listening to learn from differences and that gets you above 50 on the Conversation Meter. However, is it time for a fact-based conversation or a purpose-driven one?

We predict that living incessantly in the "What is it time for now?" question will consistently give you more timing hits than misses.

Examples of organizations asking and answering this all-important question are available online at ***thevitalityimperative.com/explore***.

Now come three ways to practice. We recommend you try each at least once and then assess the benefit to your sense of timing.

Timing Practice #1: Diagnose, predict, and prescribe

Getting timing right is a continual conversation. At Conversant, we've developed a tool called the Cycle of Value Diagnostic to help guide these timing conversations through three phases: (1) diagnose, (2) predict, and (3) prescribe. The following worksheet is a valuable resource for documenting and engaging in these conversations.

A timing practice: Cycle of Value Diagnostic

Topic:

Type of conversation		Question	Off track	Weak	On track
	Intersect	Do we have a clear contribution that is supported by data and attractive to stakeholders? What contribution is at the intersection?			
	Invent	Do we have enough creative solutions to achieve our purpose?			
	Invest	Have we allocated time, money, and talent to achieve our objectives?			
	Engage	Do the people who will get it done understand and authentically support the purpose and plan?			
	Clarify	Who is promising to do what and by when?			
	Close	Are people personally committed and producing results?			
	Review	Do our metrics help us learn and improve?			
	Renew	Do we have effective routines for identifying and making smart changes?			

Using the Cycle of Value Diagnostic, gather a few crucial participants in your *vitality imperative* and do the following:

1. *Diagnose*

  - Agree on the original purpose and results of the challenge. Write that in the top box of the form as the topic of your conversation.

  - Briefly explain the Cycle of Value: align deeply, act quickly, and adjust often.

  - Ask people to individually assess each of the eight conversations within the cycle (three *align* conversations, three *act*, two *adjust*) as on-track, weak, or completely off-track. In the margin next to each conversation ask them to write a few words answering, "What makes you give it that score?" It is important to have people first do this individually if you want the true intelligence of the group.

  - Have each person explain their ratings with the following rules:

    - Everyone listens to learn. This is not a battle over who is right. This is a chance to learn from what each other sees and believes.

    - Ask questions to sponsor a fact-based (accurate) and purpose-driven (authentic) inquiry. Accuracy questions revolve around who, what, when, and where. Authenticity questions look like, "For you, what is important about _____?" and, "For all of us, what is important about _____?"

2. *Predict*

  Have people answer and discuss these questions:

    - What trends do you see?

    - If things keep going the way they are, what do you predict will happen? Positive trends and predictions? Negative trends and predictions?

3. *Prescribe*

  Then, with your knowledge in hand, ask:

    - What is it time for *now*?

    - What are the most valuable actions to take?

    - Who is promising to do what and by when?

If you are interested in more examples of how to use the Cycle of Value to powerful effect, visit our online resources (which includes a downloadable version of this tool) at *thevitalityimperative.com/explore*.

Timing Practice #2: An adjust protocol

In addition to the Cycle of Value review, there is another way to host an adjust conversation.

Please bring your *vitality imperative* to mind. Who are the key people crucial to success? Invite them to a conversation to review progress to date and accelerate the success of your efforts. When you host the meeting follow this seven-step flow:

1. What is the purpose of our work? What results have we promised?

2. Accurately, what has happened to-date? This is a fact-based conversation: facts first, explanations second.

3. What worked well? (Always do this before you address what did not work well.)

4. What did not work well? For each thing that did not go well, what can we learn from and improve?

5. Who is there to appreciate and, specifically, for what? (Do not skip this step!)

6. What will we do to improve? These are actionable insights (e.g., "Include marketing at the beginning of the next product development cycle rather than the end"), not concepts ("We need to have better teamwork"). Who is promising to do what and by when?

7. What is our most important focus for improvement between now and our next review? Given the most important focus, what conversation is it time for now? Align, act, or adjust?

Timing Practice #3: Make the right thing easy and the wrong thing hard

This is particularly useful if you are taking on an unprecedented achievement, one that is not well-supported by historical routines, process, measures, and habits.

Once you have picked the unprecedented achievement, assemble a core group who represents different parts of the work system. Then have these conversations:

1. What important work has been hard to get done? Where has return-on-effort been low?

2. How are we making the right thing hard and/or the wrong thing easy? Unclear purpose? Lack of accountability? Processes? Measures? Cultural habits? Organizational structure?

3. What can we change to make the right thing easy and the wrong thing hard? Which of those things is it time for now?

4. With whom must we connect to make that happen? Who is promising to do what and by when?

A warning: it will hardly ever be the right time to correct everything that makes the right thing hard and the wrong thing easy. However, if you acknowledge where the difficulties are and act quickly on the ones that are ready for remedy, stress declines and the will to achieve ascends. Do this routinely and, over time, you will align your work environment with your most important, unprecedented achievements.

OK, regarding your *vitality imperative*, what is it time for now? What promises are you ready to make? How will keeping those promises strengthen community, contribution and choice?

Here are some questions worth considering as you decide whether or not you want to promise Timing in your personal and professional life:

1. Regarding my *vitality imperative*, what is it time for now? Where is it important for me to focus my energy?

2. How does timing help or hurt the connections that build *community*?

3. How does timing help or hurt significant *contribution*?

4. How does timing affect the *choice* to do great work?

5. How can I develop better timing today? What, if anything, will I do differently?

For more on timing, including the resources and practices listed here, visit ***thevitalityimperative.com/timing***.

Now, let's produce some surprising results!

PROMISE #7

SURPRISING RESULTS:

Making a Meaningful, Continual, and Energizing Difference

How wonderful it is that nobody need wait a single moment before starting to improve the world.

—Anne Frank

Success is the child of audacity.

—Benjamin Disraeli

I love taking an idea...to a prototype and then to a product that millions of people use.

—Susan Wojcicki, CEO of YouTube

In the late 1990s, Bendigo Bank, a community bank in Australia, struggled with a dilemma: major banks had shuttered more than two thousand small-town branches in order to cut unprofitable operations. Small-town officials kept calling Bendigo asking for a bank branch, but facing the same cost problems as their larger competitors, Bendigo could not agree. Their image as a community bank suffered as people lumped them in with "all the other heartless bankers."

The demise of small-town Australian bank branches had real, tangible consequences for the communities and the people who lived in them. Research found that on average locals spent $4,000 a year less in their hometown when they had to travel to a branch in a nearby city. In short, people shopped where they banked.

As a result, local businesses lost 20–40 percent of their revenue, and many were forced to close their doors. The lower revenues meant fewer funds became available for essential services, including education. The impact on small towns all over the country was devastating, and no solution was in sight.

As Bendigo continued discussions with small-town leaders and residents, they identified a major issue that needed solving: what was good for big business was not good for small communities.

This seeming truth led to an awareness of the sources of conflicts that needed to be addressed head-on.

While many small-town residents said they liked the idea of a bank in their hometown, few said they would switch banks when it opened. They were concerned about the problems and costs of changing loans and banking relationships. Additionally, many people said they did not trust the motivations of banks and bankers. They asked, "Will they just leave again in bad times?"

Conversely, internal Bendigo stakeholders were concerned about risk and did not want to invest if community members were lukewarm about a branch.

Acknowledging these viewpoints allowed both Bendigo and community leaders to come together to wonder about what could be possible and to ideate on how they could change the future they were headed to of no small-town bank branches.

Out of these talks, a new, shared purpose emerged: what is good for business must be good for the community.

What followed was a remarkable display of cooperation, grit, and ingenuity. The results were categorically surprising and relevant.

In the following pages, we'll explore how, by keeping the Vitality promises, Bendigo Bank and small communities in Australia completely transformed that country's community banking model. In the process, we'll walk you through suggested practices that you can use to help you achieve similar surprising, relevant results with your own *vitality imperative*. As such, this chapter will feel a bit different than the previous ones, and it will demand a bit more of you. Are you up for the challenge? If so, we promise you surprising results.

How Do Surprising Results Produce More with Less?

As we mentioned earlier, we think most change management approaches cost too much and produce too little impact (if any at all). Massive program offices managing the supposedly simultaneous alteration of strategy, structure, process, metrics, and rewards are a low-performance, bureaucratic nightmare. We offer an entirely different approach, if you're interested: cycles of relevant, surprising results.

Vitality grows through cycles of surprise. When people produce valuable results beyond their own expectations, there is widespread, energizing delight. If those cycles are short, valuable, and repetitive, great performance improves exponentially.

Leaders frequently ask us about building a performance culture. That is a desire shared by many, and yet achieved by few. Having witnessed many such attempts over the last thirty years, we report these two observations:

1. Organizational cultures change by shifting how work gets done, not by cheerleading, lecturing, convincing, or cajoling.

2. We can find *no* example of successful cultural change if the first visible accomplishment took longer than six months. When cultural change was successful, we have observed repeating cycles of visible results of approximately ninety days each.

It looks like this:

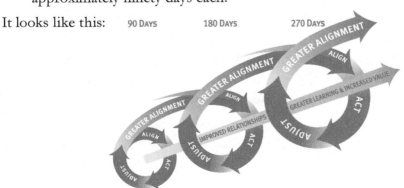

Simply put, short, repeating cycles of achievement shatter disbelief, energize employees, and accelerate improvement.

Case in point: In 1983, Lorne Whitehead, a physicist now at the University of British Columbia, published a now-legendary article in the *American Journal of Physics*. Whitehead asserted that a domino can knock over another domino one and a half times larger than itself. Each domino knocking over another one 50 percent larger than itself produces exponential momentum and, starting with one domino only a measly 5 millimeters high and 1 millimeter thick, in thirteen dominos, you can topple a 3-meter high, 100-pound domino. With twenty-nine dominos, you could topple one as large as the Empire State Building! (If you want to see a brief demo proving Whitehead's point, search online for "Stephen Morris domino chain reaction.")

Now, imagine how you can start an amazing chain reaction of performance in your organization by using similar principles and leveraging the align, act, and adjust questions in a continual cycle of surprising, relevant results.

A leader who can promise surprising results creates performance momentum that supercharges community, contribution, and choice in these ways:

1. *Relevant, surprising results get attention.* When the results matter, word spreads quickly and you refocus the attention of many.

2. *Surprising results cause people to update their beliefs.* Suddenly new things are possible and new actions are considered.

3. *Surprising results get remembered.* There is substantial neurological evidence that surprise triggers immediate emotions that make the moment hard to forget. The remembered lessons create new opportunities for vital performance.

4. *Positive surprising results energize*, planting seeds of hope that we can achieve more with less time, money, and stress.

5. *Negative surprising results* lead to some of our biggest, most durable lessons. Every enduring heroic myth and movie features that transformation of disappointment into victory.

We promise: these rapid, repeating cycles improve relationships, learning, and results.

Surprising Results Principle #1: Transform a popular problem into a 90-day core sample adventure

Core samples are minimally invasive examples of the nature of a system. For example, you can take core samples to understand soil composition and better use land for agriculture. Core sampling is used for many other reasons, including mining, oil production, and medical diagnosis. We use the same idea to design surprising results projects in organizations, and here's how:

Find an Important Problem That Seems Difficult or Impossible to Solve

Gather a small group representing various aspects of the work system. Have them wonder about what important problem you are facing, create options, and then pick one important problem with these features:

- *Relevant to a cross-section of people in your enterprise.* The small-town banking crisis in Australia touched a wide crosscut of stakeholders, from residents to community leaders to small business owners to investors.

- *Widely discussed without resolution.* The problems caused by the demise of small-town Australian bank branches were written about and discussed widely, with research conducted in New South Wales and Queensland. The impact on small towns all over the country was devastating, and no solution was in sight.

- *Capable of huge impact for many stakeholders.* Business owners, employees, politicians, educators, parents, children, and many others all stood to benefit from solving the local bank crisis.

The demise of small-town banking was surely a problem that fit all three criteria.

Enlarge the Issue: What larger problem includes the one we are trying to solve?

Find a big wall, cover it with paper, map out everything that seems related to your *vitality imperative*, and address two basic questions:

- *What happened that led to our dilemma?* Find three to five relevant causes, and then for each ask, "What happened that led to that?"

- *Who are all the people impacted?* For each group, write a few words about the nature of the impact. Wonder together about this question: What larger issue is our problem a part of?

As we mentioned earlier, Bendigo initially faced this major issue: what was good for big business was not good for small communities.

When a larger issue is identified, we naturally take into account a larger system of causes and effects. When this larger system is identified, our solutions become more effective and the population who benefits from our work increases. All who benefit, whether they know it or not, are stakeholders in our success, and each of them are potential supporters we can ask for help.

Narrow the Focus: What apparently small, 90-day success has large implications?

What's the smallest example of that larger issue that you can tackle now? This is about leverage, not just low-hanging fruit. Yes, it needs to produce a surprising, observable result quickly, but it also needs to yield actionable insight that spawns the next achievement and is useful in the larger system. Here are some criteria we've found useful:

- *Timely:* Regarding this problem, what is it time for now?
- *Engaging:* There are capable, influential people eager to work on it.
- *Measurable:* What is our 90-day observable achievement? While the project can be part of a longer-term effort, it needs to have a focused 90-day measurable result at stake.
- *Surprising:* When we say we will do it, many will doubt us. When we do it, many will be amazed.

At Bendigo, the first surprising result project was to research and design a model for shared risk and reward that Bendigo stakeholders and at least one Australian community were willing to pilot. Since the issue had been discussed to death, few believed much would come of this. They came to be surprised.

Surprising Results Principle #2: Gather support, do all it takes and nothing more

Most surprising result projects are unprecedented and poorly supported by historical strategy, structure and process, metrics and rewards, or culture and behavior. If you are not willing to provide the support needed to succeed, don't launch the project. Here is how we approach the opportunity.

Get "The System" in the Room and Troubleshoot the Challenge
Get people in the room who represent all relevant interests related to the project. This is not just the stakeholders but also the stakeholders' stakeholders. A complete, diverse group will do the best work in the shortest time with the fewest unanticipated breakdowns going forward.

You first job is to identify an authentic intersection of shared purpose that is important to all on hand. As mentioned earlier, the Bendigo project purpose was to demonstrate that, in fact, what is good for business must be good for the community. Then, align on the measurable result.

Start at the intended measurable end point, for example, "It is 90 days from today, and Bendigo stakeholders and members of one Australian community have agreed to co-invest in a pilot."

Using a big wall covered with paper, walk "back from the future" the 90-day result to the present, creating a timeline as you go. Keep asking, "What must happen right before? And right before that? And right before that?"

Stop frequently for all to troubleshoot the emerging timeline and make sure nothing is missed.

The exercise is complete when the assembled people agree that you have an accurate picture of the necessary journey.

Then, do a System Fit Assessment. A downloadable version of this tool is available online at ***thevitalityimperative.com/explore***.

A System Fit Assessment looks at the fit of your *vitality imperative* project through the lens of the existing strategy, structure and processes, metrics and rewards, and culture and behavior. We recommend that you go online to download the 10-minute assessment.

For best results, have each team member take the assessment and explain her or his ratings. Learn from the differences. Align on a group score. Pick the top ten challenges that must be met to ensure success, even if you don't do the assessment! Write the names of the challenges at the appropriate spots on your "back from the future" timeline.

Who Benefits?

Consider who benefits if you meet the ten challenges and succeed in ninety days. Write the names above your timeline. What requests can you make of the people who benefit? If they say yes, will you have the community of support you need to succeed?

Are You In?

Having confronted reality, are you committed to make this work? The triple test to confirm whether you're really committed is:

- *Community:* Are you committed to a shared purpose and worthy goal? Will you watch each other's back along the way?

- *Contribution:* Will this make an important difference?

- *Choice:* Are you each in this because you personally care?

Roles for Doing All It Takes and Nothing More

If the answers are yes, then who is taking point and coordinating all of our efforts? Who is talking to whom to gather the support we need?

Doing all it takes means you step over no relevant challenge. Doing nothing more means you do only what is necessary to launch this focused 90-day adventure. Stay lean, stay focused, get going, and learn from doing something.

At Bendigo, the core group did an impeccable job of confronting reality and made sure they had the executive support and resources needed. As they considered larger issues and the stakeholders who would benefit, a great source of support came to light: the Government of Western Australia agreed to provide dollar-for-dollar support for their project if it served as a feasibility study for how to ensure banking services for small communities.

They formed a community of contributors choosing to move forward. What lay ahead was extraordinary.

Surprising Results Principle #3: Establish a core team who will align deeply, act quickly, and adjust often

To establish your core steering team, we suggest answering two questions:

1. For our 90-day result, who must interact with whom in order to succeed? Look at your "back from the future" timeline and your list of people who benefit. Write down the names of actual people who must be involved.

2. Who are the crucial few people who can represent the interests of all involved? As many as it takes and no more is ideal, usually around eight to ten people.

Once the team is in place, use the Cycle of Value Diagnostic introduced in the timing chapter.

Have each team member answer the eight questions privately, and then explain their ratings to the entire team. Listen to learn, identify actions to take, and decide by when.

Next, create a 90-day project plan with interim milestones. Visit our online resources to find out how to do this with a tool called the Rapid Results Roadmap. A downloadable version of this tool is available online through *thevitalityimperative.com/explore*.

Surprising Results Principle #4: Enjoy the fruits of trial, progress, error, and adjustment

All of life evolves due to trial, progress, error, and adjustment. Since arguing with the design of life seems foolish, we look at *vitality imperative* projects in the same way.

Action reveals what prediction never can. Surprising successes and failures both illuminate value. A prominent product development professional from a global enterprise told us:

> *The biggest barrier we have to great new products is our own executives. Too many suffer from a "God complex" and seem to believe that they are right and evidence to the contrary is wrong. That has us stick with mediocre solutions and try to force them to work because someone in power cannot admit mistake. We have had big winners and every one of them was a function of trial, error, and improvement. Nothing works better than letting reality and real customers teach us how to be great.*

Adjust often and eagerly embrace the lessons of progress and error. Plan for adjust conversations and be ready to call for one when needed, such as when:

- You are at obvious milestones.
- Results are better than expected and you don't know why.
- Results are disappointing and you don't know why.
- Conditions change (unpredicted circumstances arrive, or stakeholders or core team members change).

During their rapid trip to a successful community bank model, the Bendigo team learned some valuable lessons.

People said they liked the idea of a bank in their hometown, but were reluctant to change where they banked. This led to the insights that people need a personal reason to change. Bendigo needed to make it easy and compelling for people to switch.

Again, many people said they did not trust the motivations of banks and bankers. This led to the insight that there was a need for a model that was viable and valuable in good times and bad.

Internal Bendigo stakeholders felt the venture was risky and were not ready to invest in a community that seemed lukewarm toward the initiative. This led to the insight that local community members needed to have a stake in the success of the branch.

Those and other lessons led to a business model, and in 1998, two communities in Victoria, Rupanyup and Minyip, embraced that model to establish a pilot program aimed at returning banking services to the towns.

The branches operated under the ownership of local people who also controlled the bank through their local board of directors. A wide cross section of the community, including residents, professionals, and business people constituted these ownership groups.

Bendigo Bank provided the banking license, a full range of banking products, deposit protection, staff training, and ongoing support. The local company employed staff and paid operating costs such as leases, wages, and utilities.

Investors in the community bank could own between $500 and $10,000 of equity. The low upper limit of $10,000 prevented small-group control of the bank and kept ownership spread evenly among those involved. The Bendigo Bank and the community branch were entitled to agreed portions of branch revenue. When the branch began to make a regular operating surplus, the local board pledged a proportion of local net profit back into their community.

When members of a community expressed interest, a steering committee of local citizens assessed community support and managed the process of bringing about a local community bank. The pledged capital needed to start a community bank was approximately $250,000. If a feasibility study demonstrated that the community bank was workable, the capital was raised and arrangements were made to open the doors of the new bank.

Any fees associated with moving loans to the new community bank were waived for a period of (you guessed it) ninety days.

The Rupanyup and Minyip branches opened on June 26, 1998. The experience was successful and spawned another rapid result: the next branch opened in the community of Upwey on October 19 of that year. The rapid cycles of trial, progress, error, and adjustment continued, and as of this writing, there are more than three hundred similar community bank branches.

The following is from the Bendigo website:

> *The number of Community Bank® branches has continued to increase each year, with customers now committing more than $26.8 billion in banking business throughout the Community Bank® network. More importantly, more than $134 million in Community Bank® branch profits has been returned to community projects and over $37 million has been paid in dividends to more than 73,000 local shareholders.*

Through rapid cycles of surprising results, the people of Bendigo inspired community members, themselves, and people all across Australia.

- *Surprise #1:* Not one, but two communities were willing to pilot the concept!
- *Surprise #2:* The branches became profitable ahead of projections!
- *Surprise #3:* Another community bank branch opened in less than four months!

Each potential community bank goes through a similar cycle of rapid results: investigation, pilot, and permanence. Each cycle yields lessons shared with all the banks and the model continues to evolve.

Surprising Results Principle #5: **Share the results and lessons widely and appreciate the contributors**

Positive surprising results elevate attitude and accelerate learning. Surprise immediately triggers emotion. In *Brain Rules*, Medina writes about how our brains respond to surprise, "The amygdala helps create and maintain emotions. . . and it uses dopamine the way an office assistant uses Post-it Notes. When the brain detects an emotionally charged event, the amygdala releases dopamine into the system. Because dopamine greatly aids memory and information processing, you could say the Post-it Note reads 'Remember this!'"

Every relevant, surprising result you share goes more deeply into memory than anything that is expected. The result is a dramatic increase in optimism for both you and your organization. Things that seemed impossible become opportunities to expand the limits of possibility. Purpose is revealed, authenticity is increased, wonder is kindled, and timing becomes clear. Silos are busted, and vitality is increased as people work together for something rather than against each other. Honestly, it's a bit like magic.

Look back at your larger issue. If you recall, the larger issue initially facing Bendigo was, what was good for big business was not good for small communities. What is your larger issue? Who else cares about it? Those are the people who will enjoy hearing about the results and lessons.

Have a Project-Closing Adjust Conversation

One great way to share results and lessons with those who care about your larger issue is to have a project-closing, seven-step adjust conversation as introduced in the timing chapter:

1. What were our original purposes and measurable results?
2. What, as accurately as possible, actually happened?
3. What worked well?
4. What did not work well?
5. Whom is there to appreciate and for what? (Capture the stories!) How will we acknowledge those people?

6. What are the actionable lessons that may matter to others? With whom will we share the results and lessons? Where and when?

7. What is our most important, longest-lasting lesson?

Share the Results, Lessons, and Stories of Appreciation

At Bendigo the larger initial issue—what was good for big business was not good for small communities—has moved extraordinarily. The group is committed to a model of community engagement and the community banks were only the first expression of that. Key lessons have been shared to broad effect.

- *Keep capital local:* Communities thrive when capital is locally derived and invested.

- *Share risk and reward:* Local owners are the most natural "net promoters." Marketing costs go down because local word-of-mouth is so effective.

- *Collaboration is key:* Co-creating solutions and cooperating to solve problems is a very different mindset than the traditional patriarchal role of bankers. It is not, "We smart bankers know best." Rather, the mindset is, "Together we are better informed, smarter, and more effective. We will figure things out as a community."

- *Values, leadership and culture* need to be true to what is good for business *must be good* for communities.

Robert Johanson, chairman of what is now Bendigo and Adelaide Bank says, "The community banks may represent only 15 percent of group profit. However, they have become the defining identity of Bendigo and Adelaide Bank."

The results are nothing short of surprising. Starting with a small research project into the viability of community banks, the trail led to two small communities of only 1,100 people, Rupanyup and Minyip. Today, David Matthews, the chairman of that first tiny community bank, serves on the Board of Directors of Bendigo and Adelaide Bank, helping to run an institution that serves much of Australia, a population of almost 24 million in 2015. That is a beautiful demonstration of the power of small cycles of surprising results to domino into extraordinary achievement. So, we reprise an image from before:

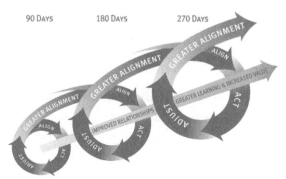

Ah, the energizing vitality of great, enduring contribution—mighty fine!

Throughout this chapter on surprising results, we have offered many suggestions for action. If you find any of them useful, please repeat them frequently; it will be good practice.

Here are some questions worth considering as you decide whether or not you want to promise surprising results in your personal and professional life:

1. Regarding my *vitality imperative*, what is the larger issue I'm facing? How might that strengthen the purpose of my work?

2. What is it time for now? What core-sample achievement can I work on over the next ninety days to create a surprising, relevant result?

3. What stakeholders can I gather to help sponsor this project? How will we work together to align, act, and adjust to create short cycles of results?

4. How will we share these results with our broader community to create excitement and further sponsorship?

5. How does designing and delivering short cycles of surprising results affect *community*?

6. How does designing and delivering short cycles of surprising results impact *contribution*?

7. How does designing and delivering short cycles of surprising results inspire enthusiastic *choice*?

For more on surprising results, including previously referenced materials and examples, go to ***thevitalityimperative.com/surprisingresults***.

OK, we've now run through the basics:

Vitality is an organizational condition wherein great results are accompanied by a threefold experience: (1) a deep sense of community; (2) reliable, personal contribution; and (3) enthusiastic choice.

Vitality leaders make and keep seven different promises to sponsor sustained high performance based in community, contribution, and choice. If you are called to be that well-connected leader, we recommend that you say the following out loud:

1. I promise presence.
2. I promise empathy.
3. I promise purpose.
4. I promise authenticity.
5. I promise wonder.
6. I promise timing.
7. I promise surprising results.

When you say the promises out loud, which ones feel confident and certain of success? Which feel less so? How the heck do you get good at all of that quickly and enjoyably? That is what the next and final chapter answers. Join us, please, for a fact-based fable.

THE VITALITY IMPERATIVE:

A Fact-based Fable

This is merely a fable. Perhaps, though, like many fables, it will be entertaining, illuminating, or both.

"People are still dying because of us…"

The words reverberated in the room like a gunshot.

"…and we are ignoring ways to prevent those deaths."

I heard the breathing of the twenty-odd people gathered in my living room. The sight of the smartly dressed guests holding wine glasses and finger foods felt odd, given the subject at hand. I don't think any of us expected to be confronted over cocktails.

Dr. Samuel Parker is a grandfatherly sort, nearing eighty, his thinning hair is completely white, and his face is marked by the lines and crevices of age. He still stands tall, his voice is strong, and his piercing blue eyes hold everyone's attention. Earlier that day he was celebrated as "a patriarch of patient care" because of how he risked his reputation and career in 1999.

"Today, you and others said many complimentary things about my career, and I thank you. However, I worry about what is still undone. You were invited here tonight because I think you, collectively, are the answer to a great many problems, and I want to talk about those problems openly as part of my handover. I'm asking that we use our evening together to make healthcare tomorrow better than it is today. I'll give you a few minutes to chat, think, and decide if you are up for such a conversation."

Sam left the room, and a buzz of discussion commenced.

"Jeff, did you know he was going to pull this?" One of the surgeons did not seem happy, and his question was directed at me.

"I knew he wanted a chance to be with all of you as part of handing his Chief of Surgery position over to me. He gave me your names specifically. Other than that, I think you should just ask Sam."

"Well, I thought we were here for jokes, toasts, and stories, not the future of healthcare. He's been talking about 'preventable harm' for years. Can't we give it a night off?" The surgeon scanned the other faces, apparently looking for agreement.

In 1999, The Institute of Medicine published a controversial and now-famous report called "To Err is Human." The report estimated that 98,000 people per year die because of mistakes in hospitals, and the medical community was shaken. Many were outraged by the claim and argued with the findings. Sam, however, said he believed the alarming news. He wrote a widely read letter to the surgical community challenging people to, "Spend less time demanding more proof and more time demanding improvement." He lost a lot of friends at the time. He had won many admirers since.

"We owe Sam a lot. If he wants an evening, whatever it's about, I'm in," said Rebecca Sterling, the head of the Medical School. She had a lot of credibility, and more than a few heads nodded in approval. Side conversations in twos and threes followed. In a few minutes seven of the twenty-one guests had left. Fourteen of us awaited Sam's return, a few wondering aloud about what we were getting into.

• • •

Rebecca and Sam re-entered the room together after a brief huddle in the hall. Rebecca spoke first.

"We have an interesting group here. Surgeons, nurses, administrators, teachers, and even, for heaven's sake, an attorney!" Win Garner, Chief Counsel for the Metropolitan Medical Center, waved at the room amid polite laughter.

"As we take up whatever Sam wants to talk about," said Rebecca. "I ask that we all keep something in mind. In today's luncheon, Sam received an important award: over the last five years, his surgical success, failure, and complication rates led all surgeons operating at our Medical Center. One of his protégés, Jeff Ryan, our next Chief of Surgery, is also in the top 10 percent. If there is anyway Sam can help bring our performances up to that level, we must seize it." Her red, curly, chin-length hair and flashing green eyes seemed an apt frame for her impassioned assertion.

"Thank you, Rebecca. I hope that our Medical School will always be led by someone who cares as much as you," said Sam in a calm, strong, easy-to-hear voice. "Let me, please, tell you what I have in mind for this evening."

"Words that we have heard hundreds, even thousands of times, can lose their meaning. I ask that we re-inspirit some familiar words tonight. Most of us here have taken the Hippocratic Oath, our profession's commitment to healing. In that oath we each said, 'First, do no harm.' I believe that means that any preventable harm demands our attention. And there is plenty to attend to."

"Since the publishing of 'To Err is Human,' much has happened. Studies in 2010 put the number of preventable deaths at around 180,000 in the USA alone. Since then other studies claim that preventable deaths could be over twice that, and I see many argue about those numbers."

"No wonder!" Ira Martin, a thoracic surgeon, interrupted. "Some of those studies count allergic reactions to medicine. How is that our fault when we don't know the allergies exist or we are not the ones dispensing the meds?"

"Ira," Sam said, "I'm here about remedy, not fault. May I ask you a question?"

Ira nodded.

"For people who genuinely pledge to 'do no harm,' is any number of preventable deaths acceptable?"

"Of course not."

"OK, let's stand there together. Whether it's 98,000 or 400,000, we're still facing an unacceptable situation, aren't we?"

"Yes. Sorry, I got a bit defensive," said Ira. "With Win Garner in the room, I don't like to admit to doing anything wrong!" That got a nervous chuckle from a few.

"Seriously, we are all exhorted to support 'open disclosure' of our mistakes," continued Ira, slowly and sadly shaking his head. "And it leads to lawsuits and professional humiliation. The ambulance chaser lawyers love to hear admission of error!"

David Jameson, the Medical Center CEO, spoke up. "Sam, we know those studies, and it is not like we aren't doing everything we can to respond. The ratings system you are at the top of is part of that. We are doing exhaustive surgical mortality reviews, and we sign up for rigorous third-party certifications. Heck, we've got The Joint Commission doing audits and certifications in the USA and Canada, the Australian Council on Healthcare Standards in Oz, and similar organizations in the UK, India, France and elsewhere. We implement every improvement we discover. What else can we do?"

"You're right, David," responded Sam. "I see more work on measures, audits, hygiene improvements, and surgical processes than any time in my career. It is important, difference-making work that I enthusiastically support. May I respond to your question regarding what else we can do?"

David opened his arms in invitation.

"I not only think that there is more we can do, I think there are also important things that *only* we can do. The quickest way I know to make sense of this is to tell you a story."

Sam went on to share an inflection point experience in his career. I'll summarize it as best I can.

About twenty-five years ago, Sam made a mistake. His mistaken diagnosis led to a cardio procedure that put a patient through considerable surgical trauma to no avail. In a break room, Sam was sharing his frustration with an equally befuddled colleague when a visiting surgeon walked in, overheard the conversation, and joined in. Soon the visiting surgeon recognized the problem, and he and Sam rushed back to the patient. Her vital signs were deteriorating rapidly. With the new information and his new ally on hand, Sam corrected the mistake, and now after several days in Intensive Care, he found that the patient was finally stable and on the road to recovery. Sam went back to that break room and wept.

"I almost killed her," said Sam. "If Brian had not been visiting from the Mayo Clinic and had not overheard us, she would have died. I'd already been practicing for twenty years…what if some of the deaths earlier in my career had been my fault, too? I was seriously considering quitting."

Brian Regan, the visiting surgeon, heard about Sam's dejection and decided to tell him about *The Truth Squad.*

Over a lengthy dinner, Brian invited Sam to join a covert conspiracy. He said that he was part of a community that met secretly once per month or whenever one of the members announced an emergency. They were a group of experienced surgeons from around the USA who had gradually inherited the conspiracy from surgeons, now retired or deceased, who had founded the group in the 1970s. One intention held them together all that time: "Being better together than we are separately."

Each month they shared new solutions and reviewed deaths and near-misses. As they did so, every surgeon became more confident, more effective, and more satisfied with their choice of career. Over the years a set of promises evolved to ensure they stayed together as a community to make surprising new contributions as they learned from one another. Brian told Sam that he needed to understand the promises before he chose to join, because they were the heart and soul of The Truth Squad. The promises were:

1. *Presence:* We give our full attention to who we are with and what we are doing. No multi-tasking.

2. *Empathy:* With curious compassion and no blame, we understand and respect each other's purposes, worries, and circumstances.

3. *Purpose:* We serve a purpose that holds us together more strongly than our differences can pull us apart: getting better every day at improving health and doing no harm. We call that purpose our "vitality imperative."

4. *Authenticity:* We trust each other with the truth. No fear or embarrassment will keep us from fact-based, purpose-driven honesty. Our trust + our differences = brilliance.

5. *Wonder:* Our best day is forever in front of us. We keep exploring new possibilities and never surrender to "this is as good as it gets."

6. *Timing:* We look for where conditions, capabilities, and our desire to contribute overlap to keep making the biggest difference possible with our time, money, and talent.

7. *Surprising Results:* Together, we discover and deliver measurable, surprising solutions that make an important difference. We will never settle for ordinary.

Sam said that living those promises with those people was the source of his success. Each of their experiences became all of their experiences. They even reviewed videos of one another's surgeries and did "peer ratings" of both technical skill and their reliability for the seven promises with their surgical teams.

"Keeping those promises forged connections that made each of us far better than we ever would have been on our own," said Sam. "To this day we differ, we challenge, we argue, and we support one another. We share breakthroughs, and we confront breakdowns. Our very different disciplines and personalities come together to make us an intelligent, effective community of medical professionals.

"Also, we saw ways to improve the entire patient experience from first visit to release from care. Surprisingly, those improvements require less time, money, and stress than previous approaches, and that is vital given the challenges facing health care.

"We now all consider the contribution our connected leadership makes as vital to the quality and cost of care," said Sam with quiet confidence. "We now think of these promises as crucial, as a *vitality imperative.*" His story had been emotional for him, and at times, for some among us.

Recently, the current Truth Squad raised an issue: their fear of lawsuits and embarrassment had kept them from making a bigger contribution. So, each member was to dare to sponsor a new Truth Squad. They pledged to one another to only sponsor diverse groups of women and men who believed in the purpose and would do their best to keep the promises. Only genuine, honorable learning communities could earn the hallmark, unflinching candor, and mutual support of The Truth Squad.

"That is why we are here tonight: for you to have an experience of what it would be like to be a 'truth squader' so that you can decide if it is right for you. I have an entertaining and educational way to do that. However, let's take another break so that anyone unwilling to explore this commitment can leave."

Animated conversation ensued.

• • •

We lost one cynical surgeon who said, "I hate this soft stuff," and a nursing supervisor who said, "Too risky for me." Win, the attorney, really wanted to stay. He was just afraid that others wouldn't trust him with the level of candor that Sam described. I encouraged him to bring that up. We were twelve strong when we began again, and I was the only one who knew what was coming.

Sam poked his head around the corner, counted heads, and said, "Would the twelve of you join me in Jeff's den?"

As we moved to the den, Sam handed everyone except me a small electronic device about the size of a triple-thick credit card. Earlier Ira had helped me put up folding chairs, a computer, and a projection screen. He spoke up. "I thought this room was going to be for viewing fond, old photos of your career, Sam. Something tells me I was wrong."

"Yes, you are right that you were wrong," Sam said.

"What we are going to do is have you participate in something we do once a year for each member of The Truth Squad. One of our agreements is that only you can tell other people you are a member. So, I am hoping that the one fellow member in the room will step forward."

"That would be me, your colleague, Doctor Jeffrey Ryan." I enjoyed the revealing moment.

Rebecca pointed at me. "Hmmm, Jeff. Is this in any way related to why your success, failure, and complications scores have all improved the last couple of years?"

I laughed. "Well, my personal, blossoming brilliance only got me so far. I've been a 'truth squader' for three years, and I've learned more and improved more than I did the previous ten."

Win said, "Is that correlation or causation?"

I responded, "If it is only correlation, then it's startling that each member has a similar story to tell. I'm going with causation."

Sam stepped back in. "You are about to get a first-hand taste of what it is like to be one of us. Every one of you has a history with Jeff. So, it is likely that you have opinions about what he is good at and bad at." That evoked scattered smiles.

"We are not doing one of our technical surgical reviews tonight. Instead, you are going to review Jeff's performance as a Connected Leader." There were a few quizzical looks.

Sam continued. "Earlier, I said there were important things that *only* we can do. Each one of you is in an influential position in the Medical Center, the Medical School, or both. What *only* you can do is to keep the people whom you influence most well-connected with our work, one another, and our patients. The biggest lesson we have learned in The Truth Squad is that the quality of connection between people is our biggest guarantee of success and our biggest defense against failure. For instance, we have seen each of our technical surgical skill improve as a function of being a well-connected learning community."

"Sam, we have been talking for years in the Med Schools about the importance of the bond between medical professionals," said Rebecca. "As well as good connections with patients and trust between medical professionals, hospital administration, and regulatory authorities. However, while awareness of the need is up, I don't see improvement. You think you can help with that?"

"Certainly, if you have people like Jeff who are serious about learning. When you get a community of capable, committed learners together, they amplify each other's strengths and minimize each other's weaknesses. Let's keep moving, and you will see what I mean."

Sam had placed two chairs together just to the side of the screen, and I took a seat in one as Sam continued.

"We are going to do a *Vitality Imperative: Connected Leader Review* of Jeff. It's based on the seven promises we talked about earlier. For each promise you will press 1, 2, or 3 on your voting card. A '1' damages the quality of connection, a '2' does not help or hurt connection, and a '3' improves connection—enhancing trust, commitment, and coordination."

"Jeff can't see who pressed what. He can only see the summary of your votes on the screen. So don't be shy. You have a choice to explain your rating or not. His job is to learn as much as he can from your experience of him. Here is a copy of the simple assessment (available for readers online at ***thevitalityimperative.com/explore***) in case you want to take notes."

We all received a document just like the one you, dear reader, will see on the next page.

A Connected Leader Review: Your Vitality Imperative

	Low	Medium	High
PRESENCE	☐ Easily distracted Talks a lot about complaints about the past and/or worries about the future Thinks things should be different than they are Seems to want to get out of this conversation and on to something better	☐ Occasional regret about the past or worry about the future Mistakes multi-tasking for productivity	☐ Feels like he or she is intellectually, emotionally, and physically with you Relaxed, focused, and attentive This is the most important place he or she could be at this moment
EMPATHY	☐ Quick to criticize and disapprove Assumes that his or her opinion or interpretation of events is valid Uninterested in why people think or behave in ways he or she does not endorse	☐ Cares deeply about and learns from people who seem to have similar values and priorities Struggles with appreciating people who are substantially different	☐ Always-on curiosity about others' purposes, worries, and circumstances Listens to learn Others always feel heard and valuable
PURPOSE	☐ Assigns tasks without explaining importance Does not like to answer questions about why we are doing something Acts as though people should just do as they are told Seems more oriented around what he or she is against than what he or she is for	☐ Responds respectfully to questions about *why* Admires purpose when it is present but also is rarely proactive about developing purpose him- or herself Equal time given to what he or she is for or against	☐ Includes others in developing valuable purpose to guide action Makes sure plans include purpose, methods, and measurable results Makes purpose the boss and thus delegates well Three-to-one ratio of speaking for purpose versus speaking against worries
AUTHENTICITY	☐ Talks about people rather than directly to people Cares more about image than substance Lies and/or withholds relevant information to avoid difficulty	☐ Honest about opinions and speaks directly to people involved Tends to assume that his or her immediate opinion is right Tries to convince or criticize anyone who resists	☐ Researches difference and listens to learn Sponsors fact-based, purpose-driven conversation Speaks openly and trusts people with the truth Cares more about achieving the purpose than being right and proving others wrong

WONDER	☐ Immediately critical of new ideas Thinking limited to past knowledge or experience Requires proof of previous success before considering a new possibility	☐ Open to new ideas when proposed by people he or she admires Rarely generates truly new possibilities on his or her own	☐ Loves the victory of possibility over probability Great faith in the creative potential of a community Known for sponsoring new, unprecedented ways to achieve important goals
TIMING	☐ Fixated on personal preferences Biased Tries to overwhelm resistance with obligation ("You should...") Overlooks relevant circumstances when trying to implement new concepts	☐ Understands the need to connect to others and circumstance Unaware when bias interferes Open to having bias pointed out by trusted colleagues	☐ Lives in the question "What is it time for now?" Moves easily between alignment, action, and adjustment as needed Enjoys finding the intersection of your view, his or her view, and the circumstances Resistance inspires curiosity rather than domination
SURPRISING RESULTS	☐ Gives people long term measures (e.g., "lower costs by 15 percent") and demands improvement Fails to consider how current habits, processes, and measures help or hurt progress Does not provide support needed for unprecedented success	☐ Includes people who must execute in designing new initiatives Does not provide the real-time support needed for success	☐ Sponsors 90-day cycles of success Helps groups representing different parts of the system to design and deliver surprising contributions Provides all support needed for high achievement Appreciates and publicizes success in the broader system

"Wow!" Juanita, a well-regarded trauma nurse, spoke up, "This feels like a spiritual MRI, Jeff! Are you sure you want be that exposed?"

"Yes. I'm a bit nervous, for sure. But I still want to do it."

"Good," Sam said. "Let the fun begin."

• • •

This exercise was confronting, emotional, instructive and, in the end, inspiring. For each promise Sam gave some indicators for low, medium, and high connection. Then they voted. Happily, someone spoke up every time to explain his or her rating. Then Sam asked for an example of someone *other* than me who was extraordinary at keeping that promise. Prior to all the comments, Sam said, "When any of you have input for Jeff, please speak directly *to* him rather than talking about him to the rest of us."

I'll give you the "Cliff Notes" version.

Dear reader: Noting what they said about me may not be all that exciting. So, to keep this interesting, here's a suggestion: think of five or six people who are familiar with you and how you work. Then, after you see what people said about me, imagine how your colleagues might rate you and how they would explain the rating. After all, if it's about you it will be fascinating!

If you do this, however, a piece of coaching from Sam might be useful. When I first did this in The Truth Squad he gave me the following way to notice my reactions to the feedback.

Sam said, "When I notice myself reacting to input, I do a quick emotional scan of six emotional families:

- *Glad: from approval to elation*
- *Sad: from disappointment to despair*
- *Mad: from disapproval to fury*
- *Afraid: from avoidance to terror*
- *Ashamed: from embarrassed to guilty*
- *Content: from relaxed to serene*

Just note the emotion, rate its intensity on a scale of 1-10, and take a breath. Then ask yourself, 'What value can I get from this?'"

This works well for me, and it might for you, too.

Presence signals

	Low	Medium	High
PRESENCE	☐ Easily distracted	☐ Occasional regret about the past or worry about the future	☐ Feels like he or she is intellectually, emotionally, and physically with you
	Talks a lot about complaints about the past and/or worries about the future	Mistakes multi-tasking for productivity	Relaxed, focused, and attentive
	Thinks things should be different than they are		This is the most important place he or she could be at this moment
	Seems to want to get out of this conversation and on to something better		

- *Low:* Easily distracted; talks a lot about complaints about the past and/ or worries about the future; thinks things should be different than they are; seems to want to get out of this conversation and on to something better.

- *Medium:* Occasional regret about the past or worry about the future; mistakes multi-tasking for productivity.

- *High:* Feels like he or she is intellectually, emotionally, and physically with you. Relaxed, focused and attentive. This is the most important place he or she could be at this moment.

My average presence rating: 2.2.
A comment: "Jeff, you are really attentive and focused most of the time as long as it has to do with a patient. With staff, though, you can seem impatient and hurried."

Extraordinary example: "Sam, even though you are the Chief of Surgery you always act like who you are with is worth your time. People far less accomplished than you treat us like annoying minions. And, in surgery, you are famous for being calm and smart no matter what happens."

Your presence rating: What do you imagine that your colleagues would say about presence?

Empathy signals

	Low	Medium	High
EMPATHY	☐ Quick to criticize and disapprove	☐ Cares deeply about and learns from people who seem to have similar values and priorities	☐ Always-on curiosity about others' purposes, worries, and circumstances
	Assumes that his or her opinion or interpretation of events is valid	Struggles with appreciating people who are substantially different	Listens to learn
	Uninterested in why people think or behave in ways he or she does not endorse		Others always feel heard and valuable

- *Low:* Quick to criticize and disapprove; assumes that his or her opinion or interpretation of events is valid; uninterested in why people think or behave in ways he or she does not endorse.

- *Medium:* Cares deeply about and learns from people who seem to have similar values and priorities; struggles with appreciating people who are substantially different.

- *High:* Always-on curiosity about other's purposes, worries, and circumstances. Listens to learn. Others always feel heard and valuable.

My empathy rating: 2.5.
A comment: "I'm a lot less experienced than you, and you are still always interested in my point of view. It's the reason I like being on your surgical team. You don't always treat hospital administration that way, though. You seem to disapprove of them occasionally."

Extraordinary example: "Dr. Hisgrove is amazing. Last week we had a complicated procedure with three surgeons scheduled to last eight hours. It took fifteen. He knew the woman's family was crazed with worry, and he went right out and sat with them, answering every question, explaining each procedure. I don't know how he could still stand up, and yet there he was being a truly caring physician. He even learned something from the family that is going to change how he explains a procedure. Remarkable."

Your empathy rating: What do you imagine that your colleagues would say about empathy?

Purpose signals

	Low	Medium	High
PURPOSE	Assigns tasks without explaining importance	Responds respectfully to questions about *why*	Includes others in developing valuable purpose to guide action
	Does not like to answer questions about why we are doing something	Admires purpose when it is present but also is rarely proactive about developing purpose him- or herself	Makes sure plans include purpose, methods, and measurable results
	Acts as though people should just do as they are told		Makes purpose the boss and thus delegates well
	Seems more oriented around what he or she is against than what he or she is for	Equal time given to what he or she is for or against	Three-to-one ratio of speaking for purpose versus speaking against worries

- *Low:* Assigns tasks without explaining importance; does not like to answer questions about why we are doing something; acts as though people should just do as they are told. Seems more oriented around what he or she is against than what he or she is for.

- *Medium:* Responds respectfully to questions about why. Admires purpose when it is present but also is rarely proactive about developing purpose him or herself. Equal time given to what he or she is for or against.

- *High:* Includes others in developing valuable purpose to guide action; makes sure plans include purpose, methods, and measurable results; makes purpose the boss and thus delegates well. Three-to-one ratio of speaking *for* purpose versus speaking *against* worries.

My purpose rating: 3.0.

A comment: "Jeff, I often use you as an example because I want our students to see what it means to stay true to a mission. For you, everything is about 'improving health and doing no harm.' Even what you complain about is rooted in that purpose."

Extraordinary example: "You are the example, Sam. Good on ya, mate, we need more like you." (Can you tell we had an Australian in the group?)

Your purpose rating: What do you imagine that your colleagues would say about purpose?

Authenticity signals

	Low	Medium	High
AUTHENTICITY	Talks about people rather than directly to people	Honest about opinions and speaks directly to people involved	Researches difference and listens to learn
	Cares more about image than substance	Tends to assume that his or her immediate opinion is right	Sponsors fact-based, purpose-driven conversation
	Lies and/or withholds relevant information to avoid difficulty	Tries to convince or criticize anyone who resists	Speaks openly and trusts people with the truth
			Cares more about achieving the purpose than being right and proving others wrong

- *Low:* Talks about people rather than directly to people; cares more about image than substance; lies and/ or withholds relevant information to avoid difficulty.

- *Medium:* Honest about opinions and speaks directly to people involved; however, tends to assume that his or her immediate opinion is right; tries to convince or criticize anyone who resists.

- *High:* Researches difference and listens to learn; sponsors fact-based, purpose driven conversation. Speaks openly and trusts people with the truth. Cares more about achieving the purpose than being right and proving others wrong.

My authenticity rating: 2.5.

A comment: "I count on you for straight talk, Jeff. You don't avoid anything and, in our history together, you sure don't lie or withhold info. There are times, though, when you get opinionated about policies without finding out why the policy exists. I'd like to see you more curious when you and I disagree."

Extraordinary example: "Juanita, I apprentice to you in this department. You are honest, and yet so relaxed and civil that people hear the truth from you easier than they can from most people. Your respectful interest has people open up to you and tell you things they don't tell the rest of us. I am grateful for your leadership."

Your authenticity rating: What do you imagine that your colleagues would say about authenticity?

Wonder signals

	Low	Medium	High
WONDER	☐ Immediately critical of new ideas Thinking limited to past knowledge or experience Requires proof of previous success before considering a new possibility	☐ Open to new ideas when proposed by people he or she admires Rarely generates truly new possibilities on his or her own	☐ Loves the victory of possibility over probability Great faith in the creative potential of a community Known for sponsoring new, unprecedented ways to achieve important goals

- *Low:* Immediately critical of new ideas; thinking limited to past knowledge or experience; requires proof of previous success before considering a new possibility.

- *Medium:* Open to new ideas when proposed by people he or she admires; rarely generates truly new possibilities on his or her own.

- *High:* Loves the victory of possibility over probability; great faith in the creative potential of a community; known for sponsoring new, unprecedented ways to achieve important goals.

My wonder rating: 2.2.

A comment: "Jeff, we have great ideas together. I like being in your surgical team post-op debriefs because you are so open to new thinking. However, there doesn't seem to be much wonder when administrative staff of the hospital is around; you could do better with them."

Extraordinary example: "Wanda Potts is wonderful. She leads our graduate teacher program at the Med School and she is always coming up with new ways for students to learn better and faster. She is an idea magnet: people shower her with new ideas; she loves it and so do they."

Your wonder rating: What do you imagine that your colleagues would say about wonder?

Timing signals

	Low	Medium	High
AUTHENTICITY	☐ Talks about people rather than directly to people	☐ Honest about opinions and speaks directly to people involved	☐ Researches difference and listens to learn
	Cares more about image than substance	Tends to assume that his or her immediate opinion is right	Sponsors fact-based, purpose-driven conversation
	Lies and/or withholds relevant information to avoid difficulty	Tries to convince or criticize anyone who resists	Speaks openly and trusts people with the truth
			Cares more about achieving the purpose than being right and proving others wrong

- *Low:* Fixated on personal preferences; biased; tries to overwhelm resistance with obligation (" You *should…*"); overlooks relevant circumstances when trying to implement new concepts.

- *Medium:* Understands the need to connect to others and circumstance; unaware when bias interferes; open to having bias pointed out by trusted colleagues.

- *High:* Lives in the question "What is it time for *now*?" Moves easily between alignment, action, and adjustment as needed. Enjoys finding the intersection of your view, his or her view, and the circumstances. Resistance inspires curiosity rather than domination.

My timing rating: 2.8.

A comment: "Jeff, this is an area of great strength for you. When it comes to anything related to patient care you have an unbiased eye for what is needed in a given moment. You constantly scan conditions and let that update your actions…very impressive."

Extraordinary rating: "Sam, your idea that it is time for surgical teams to think more like a great band than virtuoso musicians is terrific. You keep inspiring people to keep evolving so we are leading healthcare change instead of being crushed by it."

Your timing rating: What do you imagine that your colleagues would say about timing?

Surprising Results signals

	Low	Medium	High
SURPRISING RESULTS	☐ Gives people long term measures (e.g., "lower costs by 15 percent") and demands improvement Fails to consider how current habits, processes, and measures help or hurt progress Does not provide support needed for unprecedented success	☐ Includes people who must execute in designing new initiatives Does not provide the real-time support needed for success	☐ Sponsors 90-day cycles of success Helps groups representing different parts of the system to design and deliver surprising contributions Provides all support needed for high achievement Appreciates and publicizes success in the broader system

- *Low:* Gives people long-term measures (e.g., "lower costs by 15 percent") and demands improvement; fails to consider how current habits, processes, and measures help or hurt progress; does not provide support needed for unprecedented success.

- *Medium:* Includes people who must execute in designing new initiatives; however, does not provide the real-time support needed for success.

- *High:* Sponsors 90-day cycles of success; helps groups representing different parts of the system to design and deliver surprising contributions; provides all support needed for high achievement; appreciates and publicizes success in the broader system.

Surprising Results rating: 2.6.

A comment: "Jeff, the work you are doing with residents and interns to identify and implement improvements in care is making a big difference. You are turning your great sense of timing into measurable projects people love to be a part of. One critique: sometimes you get people inspired about a project without making sure they have support they need to succeed."

Extraordinary example: Win, our attorney, said, "I admire Atul Gawande. He supports rapid research and testing at places like the Institute for Healthcare Improvement. Trying out that two-minute surgical team checklist his group proposed cut death rates by 47 percent! Talk about surprising results! Who thought a check list could make that kind of impact?"

Your surprising results rating: What do you imagine that your colleagues would say about surprising results?

Well, that is the Cliff Notes version of my feedback roller coaster ride. I'm struck by how much the promises were present when we were doing this. It was a deeply appreciative, respectful, and yet confronting experience. I'm far better than I used to be, and still have plenty to learn. How about you?

• • •

"Whew!" Win was rubbing the back of his hand across his forehead. "I think my empathy skills are working because every comment we gave you caused a reaction in me!"

"Same for me," said Rebecca, holding up her *Vitality Imperative* ratings sheet. "I filled out my own self-assessment along the way…did anyone else?" There were numerous nods and waves of paper.

Sam stood up. "I am glad that you were thinking about your own ability to connect with others because it's crucial to our performance. Back when I left medical school a doctor was thought of as some all-knowing medical virtuoso. Today we have many more medical specialties, and when patient lives are at stake we need to quickly come together as a coordinated community of experts. We've got to keep getting better at the crucial capability of connection. If you think of us as a great band rather than virtuoso musicians, consider the seven promises to be the sheet music.

"This has sure been a wake-up call for me," said David Jameson, the Medical Center CEO, in a mood of quiet reflection. "If I'm going to be a great band member, the promise that needs a lot of attention from me is Presence. My hurried multi-tasking has me give full attention to hardly anything. I think it actually diminishes my effectiveness at the other six promises."

"David, what you are doing is smart," said Sam. "I think it's best to focus on one promise for a while instead of trying to get better at everything all at once. The most we've found works is Presence plus one other promise and even then you can look at them as one focus, like 'purposeful presence.' And, when the whole Truth Squad knows what each person is developing, we naturally notice and support progress. We apprentice each other's strengths and, as a community, we each improve with less time, money, and stress."

David raised another issue. "Sam, have you and your group thought about how we improve as an institution? This is great for individuals, but what about the whole Medical Center and Medical School system?"

Rebecca chimed in. "That is important to me, too!"

Sam looked to me. So, I took the question.

"In The Truth Squad we have physicians from major medical centers, commissions, and councils in the USA, Europe, and Australia. We have each tracked the success, failure, complication, and mortality rates results in our surgical teams. To a person we are experiencing less preventable harm and fewer preventable deaths than the average of the medical systems we are affiliated with. We are also experiencing higher morale than the norm on our teams. All that deserves attention."

"For the last five years we each have been asking to review surveys and other feedback from patients, their families, and our colleagues in the institutions where we work. We have noticed some patterns where measurable improvements and morale are both high. Patients and colleagues report three things: a strong sense of *community* and making significant *contribution* as a personal *choice* rather than an obligation. We have also found a strong correlation between those three experiences and keeping the seven promises."

"For the last two years I've been coordinating that research. We have developed a simple assessment you can do for teams or entire, large institutions to scan for strengths and weaknesses in community, contribution, and choice. That will tell you how urgent it is to upgrade the vitality of the connections in your team or organization. Where vitality is low, we then recommend that you look for influential leaders and teams who would like to take on making and keeping the vitality promises."

"Sign me up!" David obviously wanted the simple assessment.

Sam smiled. "I'm happy to hear that, David. We will send it to anyone who asks for it. Actually, we will only send it to those who ask because we think choice is so important to vitality. Download the assessment online and you can have it for free." In the end, our night featured many energetic discussions. We learned a lot from one another. Win Garner shared his worries about being included and got some good ideas from us non-lawyers about how to manage his involvement. Sam asked that Win, and all of us, sleep on the experience we'd shared before asking to be the newest colleagues in The Truth Squad. "Thank you, each of you, for staying tonight.

I'm honored and heartened by your interest. Think it over and, if you want to do this in the cold light of day, we would love to have you with us."

I think that evening was a much better way to honor Sam than more cocktails and a slide show. He was deeply moved, as were we all.

It has been a few months. There are now ten new squads, a total of about 500 people in a few different parts of the world. We are still evolving and now we call ourselves *Vitality Teams*. We are still working through the challenges of connecting the interests of patients, regulators, pharmaceutical companies, insurance companies, legal bodies, and so on. These are big challenges, and we are not naïve about that.

We believe that meeting those challenges with community, contribution, and choice will be more successful than fear, mechanics, and manipulation. We intend to prove that, and we won't give up. That's our promise.

*So ends the fable. We hope to connect with you again at **thevitalityimperative.com**. Thanks for sticking with us until the end.*

APPRECIATION

We admire and thank those, without whom, *The Vitality Imperative* would not exist:

To our courageous clients who believe that the vitality of people and organizational performance are inextricably linked: your confidence in connected leadership is building more sane, humane, and sustainable organizations.

To Anne Murray Allen, whose devotion to proving that wealth and well-being go together permeates our practice; Bob Johnson, our CEO, who is living proof of high-vitality leadership; Colin Pidd, who moves us and our clients to create new, astonishing solutions, assuring that our best day is never behind us; David Goldsmith, our President, for betting our financial performance on the quality of our contribution; Jennifer Simpson, for her rigorous devotion to communication and connection as a source of meaningful achievement; Robin Anselmi, for gracefully combining technical and social excellence; Tom Knighton, for proving that connected leadership is a vital, strategic asset for complex organizations; Marie Larkin, for her fierce faith in the brilliance of community; Monique Breault and Susan Burgess, for impassioned, impeccable research; Ann Shannon, for revealing the connection between empathy and extraordinary results; Mary Rianoshek and Melissa Madden for the creative ways you orchestrate time and talent to free us to explore, experiment, and write; Erica France and Katie Mingo, for wholehearted design and production; Richard Rianoshek, the co-founder of Conversant, for the foundation upon which we build; our profound thanks to Richard Moss for sharing the life-affirming power of presence as a source of vitality; and, with pleasure, we thank Jake Johnson, our muse, editor, and friend.

We gratefully salute these *Conversant* colleagues and their important contributions to *Vitality:*

Tania Anderson

Bruce Andrus-Hughes

Steve Apps

Mary Brake

Alan Brown

James Chen

Dugald Christie-Johnston

Paul Cochrane

Siobhan Cribbin

Kell Delaney

Dianne Dickerson

Sean Dunn

Dana Dupuis

Ray Eckerman

Jim Fizdale

Emma Franklin

Carolyn French

Evelyn Jonkman

Jaap Jonkman

Liam Linley

Damiao Lo

Xisca Mairata

Margaret Manchee

Juan Mobili

Magda Newman

Colin Oliver

Greg O'Meara

Jane Palmer

Andreea Pamfilie

Courtney Pullen

Nick Rianoshek

Chris Rubick

Sally Rundle

Ralf Schneitz

Paul Schrijnen

Audrey Schroeder

Harry Sloofman

Morris Taylor

Hilary Wilson

Malte Witt-Larsen

We applaud long-standing allies who challenge and enrich our work: Bill Boyar, Judy Connolly, Cade Cowan, David Dotlich, Marilyn Draper, Will Fleissig, Ike Harris, Roger Henderson, Ron Hill, Ron Meeks, Greg Merten, Peter Mulford, Jim Reinhart, Jim Rianoshek, Scott Spann, Don Van Winkle, and our friends from *The Jump* (David Pidd, Jim Lawson, Jo Zealand, et al).

It is an honor to know and learn from each of you.

Mickey Connolly, Jim Motroni, and Richard McDonald.

ABOUT CONVERSANT

We are a diverse, global community of dedicated professionals with a shared conviction: *improving human connection allows any organization to get more done with less time, money, and stress.* We research and share ways to enhance the connection people have with one another and their work that increase alignment, lower costs, and improve performance. This is work we are proud to do.

Our backgrounds include many different windows into human connectivity: negotiation, advertising, senior executive roles in global corporations, art, broadcast journalism, script writing, linguistics, acting, research & development, systems engineering, design thinking and advanced degrees in psychology, organizational communication, and learning design. We speak eight different languages and have worked in over 100 countries and 400 organizations. We have learned a lot and we will never stop learning.

No matter where we go in the world, we have found that where human connection is strong and results are extraordinary, people report three characteristics:

- *Community:* a powerful experience of shared purpose, trust, and mutual support.
- *Contribution:* people deeply enjoy making a meaningful, measurable difference.
- *Choice:* people choose to do great work rather than merely comply with the demands of superiors.

From nearly 30 years of research we have found that:

1. When community, contribution, and choice are present costs go down while collaboration, performance, and engagement go up.
2. There are learnable Connected Leader ™ behaviors that make it all happen.
3. Those behaviors develop quickly when related to relevant, real challenges.

When should you contact us? Whenever you want or need to achieve more with less time, money, and stress. If any of these *disconnection signals* are present we know we can help:

- *Community signals:* unresolved conflicts, turf protection, lack of shared purpose, poor cross-boundary cooperation, mistrust
- *Contribution signals:* unclear roles, slow and/ or biased decision-making, broken promises, ineffective performance management, weak succession plans
- *Choice signals:* defensiveness, blame, excuses, resistance to change, top talent wanting to leave, poor employee engagement

Our clients have documented returns as high as 100:1 based on actual business metrics. We have worked with people on six continents in organizations such as AMP, Australia Post, Ball Aerospace, BP, Capital One, CH2M Hill, China Energy Foundation, Cisco, Coca-Cola, DP DHL, HP, Humana, Johnson & Johnson, Lockheed Martin, Lloyds Banking Group, McDonald's, Microsoft, Mondelez, The Nature Conservancy, National Australia Bank, Nike, Port of Portland, Telstra, United Launch Alliance, US Cellular, Wynn-Las Vegas, Zurich Insurance, and many more.

If it is time for you to take on achieving more with less time, money, and stress please get in touch. If the notion of Connected Leadership™ appeals to you, please get in touch. Together, we can craft relevant, timely solutions to performance and leadership development challenges.

CONVERSANT

Conversant U.S.
1406 Pearl Street, 2nd Floor
Boulder, Colorado 80302
+1 303.541.9491

Conversant Australia
Loft 4, 41-49 Smith Street
Fitzroy, Victoria Australia 3065
+61 (0) 3 9417 6356

conversant.com

APPENDIX:
Additional resources referenced thoughout the book

In this appendix, you will see six forms many clients use frequently. Also, we invite readers who want more information go to ***thevitalityimperative.com/explore***, where materials are organized by chapter. This resource is intended to be a "reader's companion" for people pursuing their own interest in various aspects of the book. It may not be attractive or useful to people who have not read *The Vitality Imperative*.

Please let us know what you think! You can reach us via the website or at ***mickjimrich@conversant.com***.

Emotional Families Scale

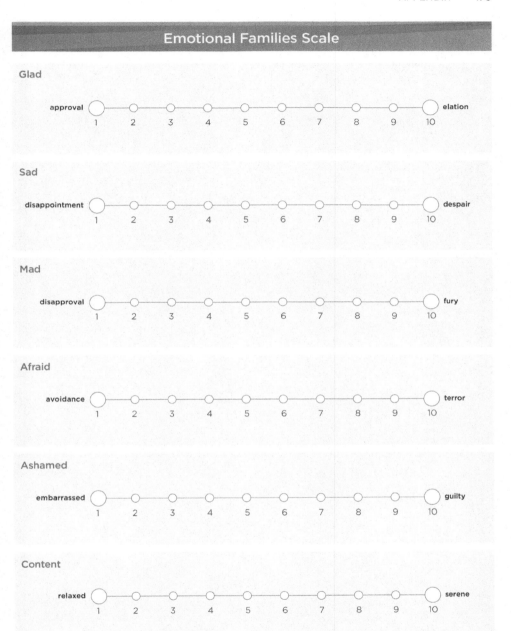

Glad

approval ○—○—○—○—○—○—○—○—○—○ elation
1   2   3   4   5   6   7   8   9   10

Sad

disappointment ○—○—○—○—○—○—○—○—○—○ despair
1   2   3   4   5   6   7   8   9   10

Mad

disapproval ○—○—○—○—○—○—○—○—○—○ fury
1   2   3   4   5   6   7   8   9   10

Afraid

avoidance ○—○—○—○—○—○—○—○—○—○ terror
1   2   3   4   5   6   7   8   9   10

Ashamed

embarrassed ○—○—○—○—○—○—○—○—○—○ guilty
1   2   3   4   5   6   7   8   9   10

Content

relaxed ○—○—○—○—○—○—○—○—○—○ serene
1   2   3   4   5   6   7   8   9   10

A Presence-Empathy Deep Dive: Keeping the empathy promise

EMPATHY \ PRESENCE	Thoughts	Emotions	Actions	Themes
Purposes (for)				
Worries (against)				
Circumstances (facts)				

©2015 Conversant

Conversation Prep Chart

Key people	Purposes (for)	Worries (against)	Circumstances (facts)
Me			
Intersecting themes			

Authentic shared purpose

Moving up the Conversation Meter

	Focus: Listen to learn	Ask questions
Pretense *to* Sincerity	Research opinions, purposes, and concerns. • Ask questions they would like to answer. • Ask questions that can't be answered by "yes" or "no."	(Name), what is your opinion about (facts)? Have you seen a similar situation? Please tell me about that. What do you think we should do?
Sincerity *to* Accuracy	Research the facts and explanations. Uncover the facts behind the opinions.	Ask the reporter's questions: who, what, when, where, and how? • For example: What happened that has you say that? Are there any other possible explanations for those facts? Which explanation is most useful?
Accuracy *to* Authenticity	Research purpose.	For you, (Name), what is important about...? What makes that important to you? What are your essential purposes and concerns here? My sense of it is _____ is important to you, is that right?
Low-end Authenticity *to* High-end Authenticity	Research the intersection. Clarify essential purpose and reveal intersections for action.	If (X) is important to you and (Y) is important to me, how can we help one another? What do we have in common? What do you think is possible? What is it time for now?

A timing practice: Cycle of Value Diagnostic

Topic:

Type of conversation		Question	Off track	Weak	On track
	Intersect	Do we have a clear contribution that is supported by data and attractive to stakeholders? What contribution is at the intersection?			
	Invent	Do we have enough creative solutions to achieve our purpose?			
	Invest	Have we allocated time, money, and talent to achieve our objectives?			
	Engage	Do the people who will get it done understand and authentically support the purpose and plan?			
	Clarify	Who is promising to do what and by when?			
	Close	Are people personally committed and producing results?			
	Review	Do our metrics help us learn and improve?			
	Renew	Do we have effective routines for identifying and making smart changes?			

A Connected Leader Review: Your Vitality Imperative

	Low	Medium	High
PRESENCE	☐ Easily distracted Talks a lot about complaints about the past and/or worries about the future Thinks things should be different than they are Seems to want to get out of this conversation and on to something better	☐ Occasional regret about the past or worry about the future Mistakes multi-tasking for productivity	☐ Feels like he or she is intellectually, emotionally, and physically with you Relaxed, focused, and attentive This is the most important place he or she could be at this moment
EMPATHY	☐ Quick to criticize and disapprove Assumes that his or her opinion or interpretation of events is valid Uninterested in why people think or behave in ways he or she does not endorse	☐ Cares deeply about and learns from people who seem to have similar values and priorities Struggles with appreciating people who are substantially different	☐ Always-on curiosity about others' purposes, worries, and circumstances Listens to learn Others always feel heard and valuable
PURPOSE	☐ Assigns tasks without explaining importance Does not like to answer questions about why we are doing something Acts as though people should just do as they are told Seems more oriented around what he or she is against than what he or she is for	☐ Responds respectfully to questions about *why* Admires purpose when it is present but also is rarely proactive about developing purpose him- or herself Equal time given to what he or she is for or against	☐ Includes others in developing valuable purpose to guide action Makes sure plans include purpose, methods, and measurable results Makes purpose the boss and thus delegates well Three-to-one ratio of speaking for purpose versus speaking against worries
AUTHENTICITY	☐ Talks about people rather than directly to people Cares more about image than substance Lies and/or withholds relevant information to avoid difficulty	☐ Honest about opinions and speaks directly to people involved Tends to assume that his or her immediate opinion is right Tries to convince or criticize anyone who resists	☐ Researches difference and listens to learn Sponsors fact-based, purpose-driven conversation Speaks openly and trusts people with the truth Cares more about achieving the purpose than being right and proving others wrong

WONDER	☐ Immediately critical of new ideas	☐ Open to new ideas when proposed by people he or she admires	☐ Loves the victory of possibility over probability
	Thinking limited to past knowledge or experience	Rarely generates truly new possibilities on his or her own	Great faith in the creative potential of a community
	Requires proof of previous success before considering a new possibility		Known for sponsoring new, unprecedented ways to achieve important goals

TIMING	☐ Fixated on personal preferences	☐ Understands the need to connect to others and circumstance	☐ Lives in the question "What is it time for now?"
	Biased	Unaware when bias interferes	Moves easily between alignment, action, and adjustment as needed
	Tries to overwhelm resistance with obligation ("You should...")	Open to having bias pointed out by trusted colleagues	Enjoys finding the intersection of your view, his or her view, and the circumstances
	Overlooks relevant circumstances when trying to implement new concepts		Resistance inspires curiosity rather than domination

SURPRISING RESULTS	☐ Gives people long term measures (e.g., "lower costs by 15 percent") and demands improvement	☐ Includes people who must execute in designing new initiatives	☐ Sponsors 90-day cycles of success
	Fails to consider how current habits, processes, and measures help or hurt progress	Does not provide the real-time support needed for success	Helps groups representing different parts of the system to design and deliver surprising contributions
	Does not provide support needed for unprecedented success		Provides all support needed for high achievement
			Appreciates and publicizes success in the broader system

CPSIA information can be obtained
at www.ICGtesting.com
Printed in the USA
BVOW07*1205070816

458228BV00001B/1/P